low carb
high flavor
recipes
made easy

Fiona Carns

bay
books

First American edition published 2003 by
BAY BOOKS, an imprint of BAY/SOMA Publishing,
444 DeHaro Street, No. 130,
San Francisco, California 94107

Originally published 2002 by Penguin Books Australia Ltd

Design by Tony Palmer, Penguin Design Studio
Typeset in Univers CE 45 Light by Post Pre-press Group,
Brisbane, Queensland

BAY BOOKS edition edited by Barbara King and Caroline Fisher
Production by Jeff Brandenburg
Cover designed by FLUX

Cataloging-in-Publication data available from the publisher

Printed and bound in Canada

10 9 8 7 6 5 4 3 2 1

Distributed by Publisher's Group West

Front cover image:
Coriander-Crusted Beef (page 101) with Green Beans and Sweet Potato and Ginger Mash (page 154, variation)
Back cover image:
Baked Pear with Almond and Coconut Crumble (page 180)

To my beautiful mother, Jan, who fueled in me the passion to cook, and my father, Keith, who made me believe I could make this happen.

Acknowledgments

Countless thank-yous to my fabulous husband (and guinea pig),
Greg, and our children, Jackson, Olivia and Georgia – for their
encouragement, support and advice. To my generous and faithful
friends who cooked, sampled and constructively criticized my recipes.
To the talented and dynamic team at Penguin: Executive Publisher
Julie Gibbs, who believed in me and this book; Kirsten Abbott,
my editor, for her clear vision and diplomatic guidance; and Tony Palmer,
for his eagle eye and slick production and design. Many thanks to
photographer Simon Griffiths and food stylist Fiona Hammond for their
beautiful work. To my trainers, Peter Ellis and Tim Schleiger – thank you
for your professional brilliance and encouragement. Thank you to the
indispensable Greg Tandy for his advice and endless assistance. And
finally, a very special thank-you to my highly efficient personal assistant
and friend, Claire Turnbull, who tirelessly participated in the preparation,
cooking and transcription of these recipes.

CONTENTS

INTRODUCTION

This is not a diet book. It is a collection of simple, healthy and tasty home-cooked meals that everyone can enjoy, especially those following a low-carbohydrate program. At first, you may be surprised at how easy and mouthwatering these recipes are, but that is the joy of cooking freely with fantastic, fresh produce and once-forbidden ingredients. Herein lies the secret to maintaining a great food program that helps you reach and maintain your ideal size.

When I left school in the early eighties, I adopted the "low-fat" lifestyle that was widely encouraged at the time. I used very little butter or oil and ate no nuts, seeds or avocado, few eggs, little red meat or fish and only a sprinkle of cheese for fear of expanding thighs and increased cholesterol. I ate bread, pasta, rice, potatoes and cereals – and I couldn't imagine life without them. Exercising regularly kept me fit and pretty trim, but in early 1999, after six months of breastfeeding my third child, I found the excess weight I carried difficult to budge despite a strict low-fat diet. I did not believe I was overeating; I was just hungry and ate to satisfy my hunger.

I was tired all the time and frequently needed to nap during the day. I suffered from indigestion

and frequently felt bloated. My skin was dry, my nails constantly split and I had a very flaky scalp.

I was not overweight but felt soft and certainly not at my fighting weight.

I discussed these problems with a friend, who gave me *Fat or Fiction* by Donna Aston.

This was my first introduction to the world of low-carbohydrate eating. Immediately it all made

sense, because the author addressed health and well-being as part of her weight-loss program.

I investigated other low-carbohydrate diets, but few inspired me to cook. Many were too

extreme and unsustainable in the long term. The food and recipes did nothing for my

imagination and little for my taste buds. I had always been a passionate cook and loved

creating high-flavored food, with influences from a range of ethnic cuisines. So I followed

the principles of the big names of the low-carbohydrate programs – Barry Sears's *The Zone*,

Dr Atkin's New Diet Revolution and Donna Aston's *Fat or Fiction*. Each of these programs advocates different proportions and ratios of carbohydrates, proteins and (good) fats, but the general premise is that carbohydrates are restricted and the intake of protein and good fats is increased. With these basic guidelines in mind, I began to create new recipes that could be incorporated into a long-term food regime. I began cooking with different cuts of lean meat, low-fat cheeses and low-carbohydrate vegetables that I had previously only gazed at quizzically at the market. I used nuts, seeds and legumes or pulses and experimented with alternatives for traditionally high-carbohydrate fare. I used intense flavors derived from fresh herbs and spices, and condiments with no added sugar or starch. The result was an eclectic mix of high-flavored, simple food that was fresh, healthy and low in carbohydrates and saturated fat.

Since 1999, my emphasis has been on "real," unprocessed food – fish, poultry, lean pork and veal, a little lean red meat, tofu, fresh vegetables, legumes, pu;lses, nuts and seeds and fresh fruit, with low-fat dairy products and the healthy fats. I have left my low-fat lifestyle behind and as a result have dropped from a size 12 to a size 8. The lethargy and exhaustion I constantly felt have gone and I no longer suffer from indigestion or that terrible bloated feeling. My concentration is more acute, my skin is not dry, my nails are harder and my scalp has cleared.

I follow no hard and fast rules for the exact ratio of carbohydrate, protein and fat in each meal. Taste is the first consideration. As a general rule, protein – lean meat, fish, eggs, poultry or tofu – forms the main part of each meal with a large serving of low-carbohydrate foods, including fresh vegetables, fruit and some legumes or pulses, and a splash of low-fat dairy products and the good unsaturated fats. The recipes

in this book are delicious, simple and nutritious without any regimented counting or weighing.

I have been living a low-carb lifestyle for over three years and I love it. I lead a hectic and demanding life and, like most people today, don't have time for complicated and time-consuming recipes. My meals must be interesting, easy to prepare and tasty. So here is a low-carb collection of delicious food for every day – that looks great on the plate and is simple to prepare.

THE LOW-CARBOHYDRATE DIET

You've heard about low-carb diets. Everyone's talking about them – because they work. But what do they mean and how do they work? All low-carbohydrate diets advocate restricting or reducing your consumption of carbohydrates so as to control the body's production of insulin. They claim that this will promote weight loss and improve your health and well-being.

Some low-carb diets simply count the grams of carbohydrate consumed daily while others consider the glycemic index (GI) of foods. In basic terms, the glycemic index is the rate at which the body digests carbohydrates. As with fats, the body digests and responds differently to the various types of carbohydrate.

Simply put, when we eat carbohydrates our body breaks them down into glucose. This causes blood-sugar levels to rise, which in turn means that insulin is produced to bring the sugar level back down. The greater the amount and more refined the carbohydrate, the higher and faster the insulin response. This seesawing in blood-sugar levels can produce feelings of anxiety and exhaustion and a hunger for more carbohydrates. Low GI food is digested more slowly, leaving you feeling fuller for a longer time, and the rise in blood sugar is slower and smaller as a result.

Not only does insulin affect the appetite, it also helps to store fat. Even with strenuous exercise, the fat-storage properties of insulin are extremely strong, making the breakdown of fat difficult. Conversely, when you eat protein the body produces the hormone glucagon, which helps release stored fat for energy.

Therefore, by restricting carbohydrates, the feeling of hunger is delayed and fat storage is limited; by increasing protein, fat use is facilitated. Health is similarly improved by eating lean protein and a wide variety of vegetables and high-fiber fruits, which are full of vitamins and minerals. As a result, this high-protein, low-carb way of eating is extremely beneficial to your general and long-term health and well-being.

On a low-carbohydrate program, the main part of your meal will be protein with a balance of low-carbohydrate foods and a small amount of mostly "good" fats. Calories are divided among these three nutrients but only carbohydrates and fat are used for energy, leaving protein for repair and construction. By reducing your carbohydrates, your supplies are diminished, allowing your body to access fat reserves.

Protein is divided into high-quality foods, such as poultry, meat, fish, eggs, tofu, cheese, soybeans and whey protein-concentrate powder, and low-quality foods (that's not to say they don't have excellent nutritional benefits), such as seeds, nuts, grains and beans/legumes/pulses. Proteins are responsible for building and repairing every living cell of the body, including the tissues in the brain, muscles, blood, hair, skin, nails, glands and nerves. They are made up of twenty amino acids or building blocks, eight of which

cannot be produced by the body but are essential for healthy functioning. The remaining twelve amino acids can be made by the body. All eight essential amino acids can be found in meat and avocado.

Carbohydrates are essentially sugars. They are broken down into glucose, which is an excellent energy source for the body. When there is excess glucose, it is converted into glycogen, which is stored in the liver and muscles and throughout the body as fat reserves. There are three main forms of carbohydrate: sugars, fiber and starch. They are further divided into two groups: simple and complex. Simple carbohydrates are sugar, honey, some vegetables, fruit (known as fructose) and dairy products (known as lactose). Complex carbohydrates include fiber and starchy foods such as potatoes, pasta, grains, beans/legumes/pulses, bananas and bread. Fiber, like fat and acidic foods, is absorbed at a slower rate and helps to maintain sugar levels. Fiber, fat and acidic foods, such as vinegar and lemon juice, all have the effect of reducing the glycemic index, smoothing out the rise in blood-sugar levels and slowing down digestion.

Fats are a great source of energy, yielding 9 calories per gram. They are essential to aid the absorption and transport of vitamins, many of which have an antioxidant effect, boosting the immune system and protecting us from disease. Fat also releases a hormone that tells the brain to stop eating (believe it or not), which explains why on a low-fat diet, the body needs more food to satisfy hunger.

But there are several different types of fat, with very different properties and qualities. Mono-unsaturated fats are found in nuts, seeds and olive oil, macadamia oil and peanut oil. These fats are believed to reduce the level of "bad" cholesterol or LDL (low-density lipoprotein) and raise the level of "good" cholesterol, known as HDL (high-density lipoprotein). Polyunsaturated fats are found in fish and vegetable oils. The essential fatty acids – omega 3 and omega 6 – are part of the polyunsaturated fat group. They are essential for good health and growth and must be obtained from the diet. Unlike other fats, the body cannot make them. Omega fats lower blood-fat levels and cholesterol, protect against stroke and heart disease and are essential in regulating the immune, digestive and reproductive systems. Omega 3 fats are found in tuna, salmon, sardines, mackerel, linseed, pumpkin seeds, canola oil and green leafy vegetables. Omega 6 fats are found in sunflower, corn and sesame seeds and in oils made from these seeds. Saturated fats are mainly found in full-cream dairy products, meat and eggs. High consumption of these saturated fats raises blood-cholesterol and blood-fat levels.

It is important to understand that not every diet or way of eating suits everyone. Even when you've done your research and made an informed decision regarding your diet or lifestyle choice, it may not be until you actually start living the life that you discover what works for you. Listen to your body, as my trainer and friend Pete Ellis advised me. When adopting a low-carb lifestyle, personal experimentation will determine how much carbohydrate you can eat to make you either lose fat or maintain your weight or to simply make you feel energized and invigorated.

WHERE TO BEGIN

Everything we eat and drink is made up of calories. We put on weight by consuming calories that we are unable to burn off. Clearly, eating too much fat is not conducive to losing weight, but while most of us have some understanding of what fat is and what it does, we have little or no idea of the properties of carbohydrates and protein.

The traditional food pyramid currently recommended by various health authorities encourages us to increase our consumption of processed carbohydrates and to reduce our intake of fats, keeping them to a minimum. However, for those following a low-carb program it's important to know precisely which foods help or hinder the process.

The recipes in this book indicate the foods you should be concentrating on, starting with breakfast and working through snacks, starters and lunch, soups, salads, main courses and side dishes, to a small but tasty dessert section. With a basic understanding of the different food groups and the effect of their consumption on your body, you will start to understand the concept behind a low-carbohydrate lifestyle and identify those foods to eat abundantly, those to eat moderately and those to avoid. The foods to avoid are not as obvious as you would expect.

The following tables list the three basic food groups – proteins, fats and carbohydrates – and give a simple guide to the most appropriate amounts to consume. (Note: There are 4 calories per gram of carbohydrate and protein and 9 calories per gram of fat.)

Proteins

Lean red and white meat, fish and eggs are the major sources of protein you will enjoy when adopting a low-carb lifestyle. All meats are meticulously trimmed of fat and if using a fattier cut for slow-cooking dishes, the fat is skimmed off the top before serving. Tofu, while not used as much as fish or meat, is another excellent source of protein and an invaluable part of the vegetarian diet. It does have more carbohydrate than meat but, bearing in mind the strong health-giving properties of soy, tofu is a food that should not be avoided. Protein powder is also considered to be an excellent source of protein. It has no saturated fat and can be added to various drinks and dishes to increase the protein component of the meal.

Enjoy	Limit	Avoid
Red meat Enjoy lean cuts of beef and lamb in moderation: 2–3 times per week – even lean cuts of red meat are high in saturated fats.	*Meat* Lean bacon, ham, pancetta and prosciutto – they are high in saturated fats.	*Meat* Processed, canned products
White meat Lean cuts of pork and veal		
Poultry Chicken and turkey		*Poultry* Processed meat with added sugar
Fish Lobster, mackerel, oysters, prawns, cod, salmon, tuna, whiting		*Fish* Canned products with added sugar
Beans, pulses, legumes (See carbohydrates)	*Beans, pulses, legumes* (See carbohydrates)	*Beans, pulses, legumes* Canned products with added sugar
Eggs The yolk is high in fat, so use a combination of egg whites and fewer yolks in omelets and frittatas.		
Dairy Low-fat cottage cheese	*Dairy* Low-fat feta, goat cheese, mozzarella and ricotta Low-fat milk	*Dairy* Full-cream cheeses Whole milk
Tofu		*Tofu* Tofu packaged with added sugar
Protein powder		

Fats

Many of the fats you will consume are contained in protein-based foods such as dairy products, eggs, lean meat and fish. The balance of the fat you require will come from essential fatty acids found in nut oils, seeds and nuts. If you're attempting to lose weight, too much fat in your diet will prevent you from getting there.

Enjoy	Limit	Avoid
Lean proteins Lean cuts of beef and lamb, pork and veal, chicken and turkey, fish		
Dairy Low-fat cottage cheese	*Dairy* Low-fat feta, mozzarella, ricotta and Cheddar cheese Low-fat yogurt Low-fat milk Pure cream	*Dairy* Full-cream cheeses Whole milk
Fresh fruit Avocado		
Eggs (See proteins)		
Nut oils and seeds Nut oils – by their very nature they are difficult to overconsume. They are essential fatty acids.	*Raw nuts and seeds*	*Miscellaneous* Processed foods that contain sugar, honey, thickeners and processed fats, such as muffins, cookies, cakes, jams, doughnuts and chocolate. Many of these foods contain dangerous trans-fatty acids.

Carbohydrates

A small selection of traditionally high-carb fare appears in a few recipes. Some breads and natural oats are used in a limited capacity in the breakfast menu for those wanting simply to maintain their size and enjoy a healthy, tasty breakfast. The body's ability to metabolize high-density carbohydrates is more efficient in the morning. A variety of crispbreads and flat breads, which are low in carbohydrates, fat and calories, are listed in the products section (see chapter 9) and are used occasionally for breakfast, snacks and desserts. A selection of the lower-carb beans/pulses/legumes are also used, as they are high in protein and fiber and are nutritiously dense. As with other higher-carb vegetables, they are teamed up with low-carb vegetables to decrease their carbohydrate density and increase their flavor.

Enjoy	Limit	Avoid
Vegetables and herbs	*Vegetables*	*Vegetables*
Asparagus, beets, broccoli, broccolini, cabbage (red, white, Chinese, bok choy, choy sum, brussels sprouts), carrots, cauliflower, celeriac, celery, cucumber, eggplant, fennel, fresh herbs (basil, cilantro, mint, parsley, tarragon, thyme), green beans, Jerusalem artichokes, lettuce (arugula, butter, chicory, endive, iceberg, leaf, mixed, red oakleaf), mushrooms, onions (green, red, white yellow), peas (green, split, dried), radishes, rutabagas, snow peas, spinach, sugar snaps, squash, Swiss chard, tomatoes (actually a fruit), turnips, zucchini	Corn, pumpkin, parsnip, sweet potatoes	Potatoes
Fresh fruits	*Fresh fruits*	*Fruit*
In moderation, approximately 2 servings per day: Apples, apricots, avocados, blackberries, kiwifruit, melons (watermelon, cantaloupe, honeydew), nectarines, passion fruit, peaches, pineapple, plums, raspberries, strawberries.	Grapes, mangoes, oranges and pears. Initially you may want to avoid these fruits completely if your aim is to lose weight. Once you have reached your target weight and size, you can slowly reintroduce them.	Bananas, dried fruit, canned fruit with added sugar or in syrup
Beans, legumes, pulses	*Beans, pulses, legumes*	
Broad beans, cannellini, Great Northern beans, lentils, red kidney beans, soybeans	Black kidney beans, borlotti, chickpeas	

continued

Enjoy	Limit	Avoid
	Bread Crispbread Flat bread and high-fiber, whole-grain bread Rye and low-glycemic-index bread	
	Alcohol A glass of wine with dinner, preferably red for its antioxidant qualities. Spirits should be enjoyed in moderation, on the rocks or with low-cal mixers or soda.	
		Miscellaneous Pasta, white rice, commercial cereals, juice (fruit or vegetable), highly processed flour-based foods (such as cookies and cakes). Foods that contain sugar, honey, thickeners and processed fats, such as cookies, cakes, chocolate, ice cream, confectionery, doughnuts, muffins, jams with added sugar.

Water

On a low-carbohydrate diet, it's essential to drink plenty of filtered or boiled water. To be precise, drink 2 quarts or 8–10 glasses per day and even more if you are exercising vigorously in a warmer climate or working in an air-conditioned office. Water is vital for digestion and the transportation of nutrients throughout the body. It assists in fat-burning and the elimination of toxins, controls the body's temperature and prevents constipation. It's fat- and carb-free, so drink up.

NOTES

- The measurements and oven temperatures given in the recipes in this book have been translated from metric measurements and Celsius temperatures and have been approximated in some cases for ease of use.

- A sprig by my definition is about the length of your little finger.

- Eggs are large-sized (2 ounces). Buy free-range eggs if you can.

- Where no size of vegetable or fruit is specified, consider it medium. Buy fresh fruits and vegetables when you can. Select them by what looks good and what is in season. (You don't have to follow the recipes slavishly.) The price of goods will reflect whether they are in season or not. Frozen, canned or packaged foods are okay when you are caught short, as long as there are no added sugars. The shorter the list of additives on the label, the better.

- Herbs used in the recipes are fresh unless otherwise specified. Store your fresh herbs with their roots in a vase of water. Cover the herbs and vase with a plastic bag and refrigerate. Change the water daily and they will last for up to one week. Better still, plant a herb garden. Wash cut herbs and dry them in a salad spinner, then wrap in kitchen paper and store in a plastic bag in the crisper.

- Buying organic products sounds like a great idea (although they don't always look great), and the taste of certain organic foods is far superior to the non-organic variety, but cost and availability are considerations. I buy organic when I can, in particular free-range, organic meat and chicken that is chemical- and hormone-free. More organic products, including meat, are hitting the supermarket shelves daily, making them more readily available.

- Salt is a problem for many people as excessive amounts can cause an increase in blood pressure and the risk of stroke and heart disease. I love the texture and taste of sea salt. It is expensive, but the intense flavor generally means you don't have to use as much. Lite salt, a low-sodium salt, is a good alternative to regular salt and is recommended by doctors, dieticians and naturopaths unless you suffer from kidney disease or are diabetic.

- With such a huge variety of oils on the market, there is much confusion over which type and how much to use. I try to use cold-pressed oils as much as possible. They are the most unrefined oils, retaining all their nutritional benefits. Cold-pressed olive oil, is loaded with hormones, enzymes, nutrients and antioxidants and is also an excellent source of monounsaturated fats. Olive oil can be heated to higher temperatures than other oils and does not create dangerous side products in the way animal and vegetable fats do. It reduces the risk of heart disease because it increases the elasticity of arteries, and is anti-carcinogenic. As yet you can't buy cold-pressed olive oil in spray form, so you will need a brush and small dish for basting or decant the oil into an oil-atomizer spray container. These are available at most kitchenware stores and allow you to experiment with adding different herbs for infused flavor.

- Tamari is a soy sauce naturally brewed from whole soybeans. Unlike soy sauce it has no wheat flour and has a deeper flavor without the strong, salty taste. It is more expensive than soy but worth it and can be interchanged with light soy.

- Nuts and seeds feature significantly in this book. To dry toast or roast seeds or nuts for each recipe can be a little laborious, so dry toast them in a non-stick frying pan, shaking regularly, or dry roast in a hot oven in large quantities to save time. Keep nuts and seeds in an airtight jar in the fridge to avoid deterioration, and they should last for at least a month.
- Wheat germ and oats can turn rancid, so it's best to keep them refrigerated.
- I've included recipes for many basic standbys, such as roasted tomato sauce, chicken stock and pesto, but if time is short they can be purchased. Homemade and commercial products are available at supermarkets, markets and good delicatessens. Just read the labels carefully.
- Don't be a slave to the ingredients! If you don't like garlic, either don't use it or reduce the quantities. If you don't like coriander, try a different fresh herb. If asparagus doesn't cut it for you, find a vegetable that does. When changing vegetables, try to use a similar color, shape and texture to the one in the recipe.
- In a commercial kitchen, meat can only legally be out of the fridge 20 minutes prior to cooking. Whether this is enough time to bring your meat to room temperature is questionable – if it is at room temperature, you will reduce shrinkage and increase tenderness. The colder the meat, the greater the "shrinkage" factor.
- Keeping meat warm after cooking doesn't mean in a warm oven, as this will continue to cook the meat. Simply cover with several tea towels.
- Where options for cooking equipment are provided, the first is preferable. I always prefer a non-stick griddle pan to a non-stick frying pan as the meat or vegetables are elevated a little from the fat.
- Cooking times will vary from oven to oven and microwave to microwave. Further variations will occur depending on the cut of meat and the size of the vegetables. Cooking times are a good guideline but factor in your knowledge regarding your own oven and microwave.

Health warning

This is a cookbook, not a diet book. If you or one of your family members has a pre-existing health condition, is on medication or has specific dietary requirements, you should consult your doctor, physician, dietician or specialist prior to significantly changing your diet.

Kitchen essentials

There are a few items that are extremely handy in a low-carbohydrate kitchen, or any kitchen for that matter:
- a set of good-quality knives in a knife block with a steel (which ideally you would use before every preparation)
- nylon cutting boards of different sizes
- a zester, to give you fine ribbons of orange, lemon or lime peel that can be added to sauces, marinades and desserts
- a hand-held shredder, to give you beautifully fine vegetables and cheese for slaw and salads
- a hand-held blender – a must for morning shakes, soups, sauces and mashes

- a Japanese porcelain ginger grater or a small wooden one, to grate this notoriously difficult root (it's worth the investment, as bottled varieties of grated ginger don't come close)
- a silicone baking mat, which can be used for every type of baking. (it is easier to use than parchment paper and halves washing-up time; I use a silicone baking mat, available at specialty cooking stores or chefs' supply shops), and which you can cut to fit the shape of your tray
- a good selection of non-stick frying pans, baking dishes and trays
- a large cast-iron/enameled casserole dish – ideal for quick-prep, slow-baking dishes
- a non-stick griddle pan or barbecue grill – used constantly and certainly worth the investment
- a simple steamer
- an omelet maker – the perfect omelet is created without fear of burning or of destroying when flipping
- a good-quality salad spinner (I have two on the go continually; keeps your greens washed, crisp and ready-for-action in the fridge)
- kitchen gloves, for preparing all those chile and beet dishes.

KIDS

Although your guidance and preferences will help form your child's eating habits from an early age, you can lead children to the dinner plate but you can't make them eat. Let's face it, most kids love white bread, pasta and rice. Over time you may be able to reduce their intake of and love for these nutritionally deficient foods by introducing a wider variety of lean protein and vegetables, fruits, nuts and seeds. Encourage them to try different foods, no matter how taxing it may seem. Persist with a variety of colors, textures and flavors and invite them to participate in the preparation and cooking process to spark their interest in different foods.

When cooking for children, purchase products as raw and unprocessed as you can find. Choose food without added sugar, starch, artificial flavorings or colorings. High-fiber, whole-grain bread or whole-meal or rye bread is quickly accepted by fussy white-loaf kids when there is no alternative, but be careful of switching to high-fiber products overnight as it may take several months for their bodies to adapt. As a general rule of thumb, use full-cream dairy products and yogurt with *acidophilus bifidus casei*. If the desserts or shakes need sweetening, add maple syrup, honey or a sprinkle of raw sugar. Add brown rice, pasta or potatoes to the protein component of a child's meal, but always offer a combination: parsnip, pumpkin and sweet potato chips combine fairly inconspicuously with potato.

When cooking for the family I frequently prepare or serve two separate meals – one for the kids and one for my husband and me and whoever else happens to drop in. But this is quite incidental to my adoption of a low-carb lifestyle – eating at 5.30 or 6.00 P.M. has never really appealed. With a little organization you can share common ingredients and often the main protein component of the meal. For example, serve Bolognese sauce on pasta for the children, but spoon the sauce over baked eggplant slices or sautéed shredded cabbage for yourself.

If using the recipes in this book for your children, be guided by the kid-friendly sign ☠.

BREAKFAST

What is breakfast without cereal and toast? So many things! A fabulous low-carb breakfast is a vital meal. It requires a little extra effort – but it is worth it. Poached eggs, omelets, smoked salmon, smoothies and sausages are just some of the low-carbohydrate staples, and with a few simple ingredients you can create a sustaining, tasty meal. Eggs – scrambled, poached or soft boiled – are the main players for hot options and, together with a variety of vegetables, herbs and cheeses, the combinations are endless. The smoothie or shake with protein powder, fruit and added fiber is another great kick-start to the day. Choose fresh ingredients that are in season and experiment with different combinations. Beware – many "low-fat" breakfast items are in fact full of carbohydrates. For example, just one glass of fruit juice, although low in fat, could contain enough carbohydrates to make up your daily allowance. (If you can't go without some form of fruit, eat a whole piece instead to receive the added benefits of the fiber. Avoid bananas and mangoes, which are high in carbohydrates, and stick to stone fruit and berries.)

Similarly many commercial cereals and breads, while often low in fat, are highly processed, extremely high in carbohydrates and low in protein. If you can't abandon high-carb food altogether, the morning is the best time to include it, as this is when your body can metabolize carbohydrates most effectively. When you are maintaining your weight or you simply want to adopt a healthier diet, you can have a little high-fiber whole-grain bread, rye bread, barley flat bread, some crispbreads or corn chips as a base for eggs, salmon or sugar-free spreads. High-fiber, whole-grain and rye breads have a low-glycemic index, which makes them suitable for occasional inclusion in a low-carb diet, but after weeks without bread you'll be surprised how indifferent you become to it.

Breakfast is a very flexible meal because there are so many great alternatives. Have a shake or smoothie when you're on the run and enjoy the cooked dishes when you can actually sit down for five minutes to enjoy them.

RASPBERRY SHAKE

SERVES 1

prep time: 2 minutes

- **½ cup fresh or frozen raspberries**
- **3 tablespoons protein powder**
- **2 tablespoons whole-milk berry yogurt**
- **1 handful ice (optional – if using frozen berries, there is no real need)**
- **1 tablespoon linseed, sunflower seed and almond mixture (LSA)**
- **¼ cup water**
- **¼ cup low-fat milk**

Place all ingredients in a high-sided bowl and blend or process until smooth. Serve in a tall glass.

Note The sweetness of the shake will vary depending on the combination of fruit. If you need additional sweetness, add more fruit or a teaspoon pure maple syrup or apple juice concentrate. A sprinkle of an approved sweetener such as Splenda is another alternative. Although it's artificial and therefore not ideal, it has far fewer carbohydrates than maple syrup or apple juice. See picture of this drink opposite page 27.

Variations For different colors and flavors, use blueberries, blackberries or strawberries or any combination. Add 2 teaspoons flaxseed oil (also known as linseed) for an extra serving of omega 3 and 6 fatty acids or 1 tablespoon wheat germ, referred to as a "powerhouse" food, as it is not only an excellent source of fiber and protein but contains numerous vitamins and minerals, including essential fatty acids. These variations can be added to any of the drink recipes on the following pages.

kid friendly

PINEAPPLE, WATERMELON AND MINT CRUSH

prep time: 2 minutes

1	cup freshly chopped pineapple (no core)
1	cup freshly chopped watermelon
3	tablespoons protein powder
2	tablespoons low-fat plain yogurt
1	handful mint
1	handful ice (optional)
1	tablespoon linseed, sunflower seed and almond mixture (LSA) (optional)

Place all ingredients in a high-sided bowl and blend or process until smooth. Serve in a tall glass.

Note   When watermelon and pineapple are out of season, use 2 cups canned pineapple in natural juice or 1 cup pineapple with $^1/_2$ cup strawberries. See picture of this drink opposite page 27.

🌹 *kid friendly* without the mint.

PEACH SMOOTHIE

SERVES 1

prep time: 5 minutes

½	**ripe peach**
3	**tablespoons protein powder**
2	**tablespoons low-fat plain yogurt**
1	**tablespoon linseed, sunflower seed and almond mixture (LSA)**
¼	**cup water**
¼	**cup low-fat milk**
	pinch of cinnamon or freshly grated nutmeg
1	**handful ice (optional)**

Place all ingredients in a high-sided bowl and blend or process until smooth. Serve in a tall glass.

Note   If fresh peaches are unavailable, use canned peaches in natural juice. This will increase the sweetness of the drink and you won't need to add any form of sweetener. See picture of this drink opposite page 27.

Variations   Add a pinch of ground ginger for its medicinal properties; it's good for digestion, circulation and warding off colds. Use 4 tablespoons fresh mango instead of peaches – the smoothie will be a little higher in carbs, but it makes a delicious change. (See also variations on page 14.)

🏵 *kid friendly*

CREAMY PORRIDGE AND MAPLE SYRUP

prep time: 2 minutes

cook time: 1–2 minutes

½	cup natural rolled oats (about 1½ ounces)
⅓	cup water
⅓	cup low-fat milk
	pinch of salt
2	tablespoons whole milk
2	teaspoons pure maple syrup

Mix oats, water, low-fat milk and salt in a small saucepan and cook over medium heat for 2 minutes, stirring constantly. When cooked, tip into a bowl, pour over full-cream milk and drizzle with maple syrup.

Note With over 20g carbohydrates for the oats alone, this is not really a low-carb meal, but if you've reached your ideal size or are successfully reducing weight or just want a nutritious meal, the occasional bowl of porridge is a delicious, healthy change from shakes and eggs. After all, it's unprocessed with no added sugar, is high in soluble fiber and leaves you feeling full and satisfied for hours. If you are experiencing cramps or muscle spasms and twitching, you may be low in magnesium, which is found in abundance in oats. The maple syrup, while not strictly low-carb, does contain the trace mineral zinc, which assists in fighting infections and with the growth and repair of tissue. Use apple juice concentrate for a lower-carbohydrate alternative to maple syrup and receive the benefits of the additional fiber and vitamin C.

LOW-CARB SWISS MUESLI, SHREDDED APPLE AND ALMONDS

SERVES 2

prep time: 2 minutes

cook time: 5 minutes

1	**cup natural rolled oats (about 3 ounces)**
2	**tablespoons wheat germ**
1	**cup low-fat milk**
1	**sweet red apple, shredded**
2	**tablespoons slivered almonds**
1	**teaspoon pure maple syrup**

The night before, place oats and wheat germ in an airtight container and cover with low-fat milk. Refrigerate. The next day preheat oven to 425°F. Place almonds on a non-stick tray or tray lined with parchment paper and bake for 5 minutes or until golden. Meanwhile place soaked oats in individual bowls with apple over the top. Sprinkle with baked almonds and drizzle over maple syrup.

Note   Natural oats have the husk removed during milling but not the germ. As a result the protein and oil content is quite high. They are high in fiber, which will help prevent constipation and hemorrhoids and may even lower blood cholesterol and help prevent bowel cancer.

Variations   Use LSA instead of almonds. If you're watching every carb but still need some sweetness, you may have to resort to replacing maple syrup with Splenda. For a different taste and texture, sprinkle with 2 tablespoons crumble mixture (see page 19).

STRAWBERRY AND YOGURT WITH ROASTED MUESLI CRUMBLE

SERVES 2

prep time: 5 minutes

cook time: 10–15 minutes

4	tablespoons protein powder (optional)
1	cup low-fat berry yogurt
1½	cups strawberries, quartered
	pure maple syrup (optional)

Muesli Crumble

2	tablespoons shredded coconut
3	tablespoons raw oats
2	tablespoons wheat germ
2	tablespoons mixed raw sunflower and sesame seeds
1	tablespoon slivered almonds
1	teaspoon ground cinnamon

Preheat oven to 425°F. To make the muesli crumble, place all ingredients on a non-stick tray lined with parchment paper. Bake for 10–15 minutes or until golden brown. Mix protein powder into yogurt.

Divide half the yogurt evenly in clear glasses and scatter with half the strawberries. Sprinkle about 2 tablespoons crumble over strawberries, then repeat with remaining yogurt, strawberries and crumble. Drizzle with a little maple syrup.

Note   Increase the quantity of the crumble and store excess in an airtight container for up to 1 month. Wheat germ, sunflower seeds and almonds are excellent sources of vitamin E, a fat-soluble vitamin and strong antioxidant, which has excellent healing properties and prevents scarring.

Variations   Use LSA (but do not bake) or pumpkin seeds instead of sesame seeds. Replace strawberries with any combination of berries, or combine with passion fruit, kiwifruit, peach, pineapple or cantaloupe. It's also delicious with stewed plums (see page 182).

PEACH, COTTAGE CHEESE AND MINT

prep time: 5 minutes

cook time: 5 minutes

1	**tablespoon slivered almonds or LSA**
4	**tablespoons cottage cheese (low in salt or sodium)**
1	**ripe peach, halved and stoned**
1	**tablespoon freshly chopped mint**
1	**teaspoon pure maple syrup**

Preheat oven to 425°F. Place almonds on a non-stick tray or tray lined with parchment paper and bake for 5 minutes or until golden. Spoon 2 tablespoons cottage cheese into each peach half. Sprinkle with almonds and mint and drizzle with maple syrup.

Note If you're using bottled or canned fruit (about 4 ounces) in natural juice without added sugar, forget the maple syrup.

SHAVED TURKEY, TOMATO AND RED ONION OMELET

SERVES 1

prep time: 5 minutes

cook time: 4–5 minutes

1	**ripe tomato**
1	**egg**
2	**egg whites**
2	**teaspoons water**
1	**handful flat-leaf parsley, finely chopped**
	sea salt
	cracked pepper
	olive oil spray
¼	**red onion, finely chopped**
1	**small handful shaved turkey breast (about 2 ounces)**
2	**tablespoons grated low-fat Cheddar cheese**

Cut tomato in half, scoop out seeds and finely chop. Whisk egg, egg whites and water. Combine with parsley and half the chopped tomato. Season with salt and pepper. Heat a small non-stick frying pan (8-inch) over medium heat (or heat omelet maker) and spray with olive oil when hot. Add onion and cook for 1–2 minutes. Add egg mixture and spread evenly over base of pan. Cook for 1–2 minutes or until little liquid is left. Place turkey and cheese on one half of the omelet. Use a spatula to fold omelet in half so that turkey and cheese are covered.

To serve, slide onto a plate and top with remaining tomato and more cracked pepper.

Note   If using an omelet maker, you will have enough mixture for 2 omelets.

SERVES 1

prep time: 5 minutes

cook time: 4–5 minutes

2	strips bacon
1	egg
2	egg whites
2	teaspoons water
	olive oil spray
1	small handful spinach
2	tablespoons grated low-fat Cheddar cheese or low-fat mozzarella
	sea salt
	cracked pepper

Trim any visible fat from bacon and chop into $3/4$-inch squares. Whisk egg, egg whites and water. Heat a small non-stick frying pan (8-inch) over medium heat (or heat omelet maker) and when hot, spray with olive oil. Add bacon and cook for 1 minute. Add egg mixture, spreading it evenly over base of pan. Cook for 1–2 minutes or until little liquid is left. Place spinach on one half of the omelet and sprinkle with cheese. Use a spatula to fold omelet in half so that spinach is covered.

To serve, slide onto a plate and season with salt and pepper.

Note   If fresh spinach is unavailable, use $1/3$-cup frozen spinach, thawed.

Variation   Instead of using bacon and cheddar cheese, add a small handful of shaved turkey or 2 handfuls cilantro and basil to egg mixture, with 2 tablespoons Parmesan, for a different flavor.

☘ kid friendly

POACHED EGG STACK WITH SPINACH AND MOZZARELLA

SERVES 1

prep time: 5 minutes

cook time: 5 minutes

1	egg
2	handfuls baby spinach leaves
1	slice whole-grain, high-fiber bread
	a scrape of butter or avocado
1	tablespoon grated low-fat mozzarella

Place $3/4$-inch water in a small frying pan over medium to high heat and bring to the boil. Break egg into boiling water and poach until white is solid. Meanwhile, place spinach and a splash of water in a saucepan over medium to low heat, covered. Cook for 2–3 minutes or until spinach has wilted and remove from heat. Toast bread, then spread with butter.

Squeeze spinach to remove excess liquid, and arrange on toast with egg on top. Sprinkle with cheese and serve.

Note   If you're trying to lose weight, this breakfast is recommended only as an occasional treat because the bread, with over 10g carb per slice, puts this meal at the upper end of a low-carb scale. If you're at the size you want to be, you can enjoy light, healthy, tasty breads regularly for breakfast: whole-meal or rye made from unbleached flour, with no added sugar and labeled "low GI." If you're just craving a bit of crunch, try corn chips for less than half the carbs of bread.

Eggs poach a lot better when they're at room temperature, so remove them from the refrigerator the night before. Egg yolks, Cheddar cheese, whole-grain bread and spinach are all good sources of the trace mineral chromium, which will help to burn carbohydrates and fat.

Variation   Soft boil egg (place egg in warm water, bring to the boil and boil for 3 minutes), then peel and cut in half. Place 2 slices lean bacon on top of spinach. Spread 1 tablespoon avocado over bacon and place egg halves on top.

🌼 *kid friendly* served with lean bacon instead of spinach.

SCRAMBLED EGGS WITH DILL AND SMOKED SALMON

prep time: 5 minutes

cook time: 2 minutes

3	**eggs**
1	**egg white**
¼	**cup low-fat milk**
1	**handful dill, finely chopped**
	olive oil spray
1	**teaspoon butter**
4	**tablespoons smoked salmon, finely chopped (optional)**

Combine eggs, egg white, milk and dill, reserving a little for garnish, and lightly whisk. Heat a small non-stick frying pan (8-inch) over medium heat. When hot, spray with oil and add butter. When butter starts to sizzle, add egg mixture. Reduce heat and allow to set for about 1 minute. Gently run a wooden spoon around the edge of pan, dragging cooked egg mixture into the middle and allowing uncooked mixture to fill the pan. Repeat until all mixture is cooked.

To serve, place scrambled eggs in pasta bowls and sprinkle with smoked salmon and remaining dill.

Variations This is just as delicious with chives instead of dill. I find the addition of the salmon a little rich, so for a lighter version finely chop a tomato and mix with remaining dill. Sprinkle over scrambled eggs.

SMOKED SALMON AND CREAM CHEESE ON RYE

SERVES 1

prep time: 1 minute

cook time: 2 minutes

1	**slice rye bread**
2	**teaspoons light cottage and cream cheese blend**
2	**ounces smoked salmon**
	lemon juice
	cracked pepper
1	**tablespoon finely chopped dill**

Toast or use fresh rye and spread with cream cheese blend. Place salmon on top, add a little squeeze of lemon juice and sprinkle with cracked pepper and dill.

Note   This breakfast is higher in carbohydrates with the addition of bread. Enjoy occasionally if you're trying to lose fat and if you're at the size you want to be, incorporate low GI bread into your weekly diet as part of your maintenance program.

Variation   Use 3 tablespoons cottage cheese instead of cream cheese blend and serve with grilled tomato halves instead of smoked salmon.

AVOCADO, SMOKED SALMON AND BACON

SERVES 2

prep time: 2 minutes

cook time: 5 minutes

2	tomatoes or 4 cherry tomatoes
4	strips lean bacon
	olive oil/olive oil spray
4	ounces smoked salmon
½	avocado, sliced
2	tablespoons fresh whole-milk ricotta
8	mini crispbreads (optional)
	cracked pepper
	a few sprigs dill, basil or parsley

Cut tomato in half horizontally. Trim excessive fat from bacon. Heat a non-stick griddle or frying pan over medium to high heat. When hot, brush or spray with olive oil and add bacon and tomato. Cook for 1–2 minutes each side.

To serve, stack salmon with avocado and place on the side of the plate. Dollop ricotta on the plate and season with cracked pepper. Arrange tomatoes next to salmon with bacon on top and scatter over dill.

Note   This breakfast is higher in fat than other meals but it is mostly good fat so enjoy – but not every day. To save 4g carb, forget the crispbreads. See picture of this dish opposite.

Variations   Add a couple of handfuls of fresh baby spinach or 2 large portabello or field mushrooms, cut into thick slices and sautéed. Use low-fat cottage cheese instead of ricotta for a higher protein, lower-fat alternative. A piece of barley flat bread cut into 4 squares and baked for 5 minutes at 400°F makes a delicious light and crunchy alternative to crispbreads, but it does have double the carbs (10g).

Overleaf: Roasted Beet Dip (page 35) with baby cornichons, mini crispbreads and baby romaine

MINI PORK SAUSAGES, TOMATO AND MUSHROOM

SERVES 4

prep time: 15 minutes (prepare the night before if you have time, and refrigerate)

cook time: 10–15 minutes

	olive oil/olive oil spray	**Pork Sausage**	
2	large tomatoes	2	lean bacon strips
4	large field mushrooms, stems removed	¾	pound lean ground pork
		3	tablespoons grated Parmesan
2	tablespoons Parmesan shavings	2	tablespoons tomato paste
	sea salt	1	teaspoon Worcestershire sauce
	cracked pepper	2	cloves garlic, minced
		1	handful flat-leaf parsley, finely chopped
		1	handful chives, finely chopped

Trim all visible fat from bacon and chop finely. Combine with pork, cheese, tomato paste, Worcestershire sauce, garlic and herbs and mix well. Season with salt and pepper. Place 2–3 tablespoons mixture in your palm and make oval finger-length sausages. Heat a large non-stick frying pan over medium to high heat. When hot, brush or spray with olive oil and add sausages. Reduce heat and cook for 2–4 minutes each side or until cooked through. Slice tomatoes in half horizontally and add tomatoes and mushrooms to pan. Cook for 2–3 minutes each side.

To serve, place mushrooms on the side of plate, stack tomato on top and sprinkle with Parmesan shavings. Season with salt and pepper and arrange sausages alongside.

Note Excess sausages make a great lunch the next day served with tomato sauce or chutney and a green salad.

Variation Use lean ground veal or chicken instead of ground pork. Lean, skinless chicken sausages, with no added bread crumbs or sugar, can be purchased from a butcher and some supermarkets, and make a quick, easy substitute.

🌑 *kid friendly* without the mushrooms and tomatoes but with tomato sauce.

Previous page: Smoked Salmon and Horseradish Cream Rolls (page 31) with Prosciutto, Fresh Fig and Goat Cheese (page 33)
Opposite: Raspberry Shake (page 14), Pineapple, Watermelon and Mint Crush (page 15) and Peach Smoothie (page 16)

SNACKS
and STARTERS

A snack should be exactly how it sounds – delicious, quick and easy-to-prepare. Snacks are a big

concern for most people watching their weight, but here you'll find some invaluable ideas for an

instant fix. This chapter also contains tasty recipes for starters, lunches and light suppers, which

make great snacks as leftovers the following day. Even when you're being very strict about your

intake, it's a good idea to have a little something around mid-morning and again in the mid-afternoon.

This keeps your energy levels up and blood-sugar levels stable, and means that you won't jump

on your food at mealtimes. Another good tip when you're feeling peckish is to drink a large glass

of filtered water, as thirst is often mistaken for hunger. Then if you are still hungry consider

some of the following snacks. Instant gratification includes the lettuce leaf, and romaine, iceberg

or Belgian endive can double as a wrap for an endless variety of lean protein, low-fat dairy and

vegetable combinations. Simply place the filling in the middle of the leaf and roll it up. Try a dollop

of low-fat tzatziki (cucumber and mint yogurt sauce) on some tuna with sliced cherry tomato;

a piece of shaved turkey with avocado; smoked salmon with light cottage/cream cheese and baby cornichons; or a slice of light ham with Cheddar cheese and a dab of mustard. Sliced cucumber, radish and crispbreads also make excellent bases for snacks.

When planning your meals on a low-carb program, consider variety in your daily intake. If you've had eggs for breakfast, stay away from the egg rolls or frittatas for lunch as the yolks are high in fat. The pizza roll-ups, while simple and delicious, are for an occasional treat and should not be eaten daily. The base is low in carbohydrate in comparison to your average pizza, but it still has 10g carbohydrates for 3 slices. The toppings contain some saturated fat and don't have the dose of protein other dishes contain. It is all about balance and variety.

Many of the recipes in this chapter can be easily adapted for casual entertaining. Serve prosciutto, fresh fig and goat cheese with a drink as pre-dinner nibbles or slice the frittata into bite-sized pieces and stick toothpicks into each square to serve at any occasion.

JAPANESE SALMON SUSHI ROLLS

SERVES 2

prep time: 5 minutes

cook time: 2 minutes

2	tablespoons whole egg mayonnaise
4	sheets nori (seaweed)
4	ounces raw salmon, cut into $\frac{3}{4}$-inch lengths
2	tablespoons pickled ginger, finely sliced
$\frac{1}{4}$	avocado, finely sliced into thin strips
$\frac{1}{2}$	English cucumber, finely sliced into thin strips
1	teaspoon wasabi
2	tablespoons light soy sauce

Egg Rolls (makes 4 rolls)

4	eggs
4	teaspoons water
	olive oil/olive oil spray

To make egg rolls, lightly beat eggs and water. Heat a 10-inch, non-stick frying pan over medium heat. Lightly spray with oil and pour half the egg mixture into pan. Cook for 1 minute or until set. Gently lift edges and flip. Cook for a further 10 seconds, then gently slide onto a plate. Repeat with remaining mixture.

Place cooked egg rolls on a cutting board and spread with a little mayonnaise. Place a nori sheet over each roll and evenly distribute salmon strips across the middle of each sheet. Layer ginger, avocado and cucumber strips on top of salmon and carefully roll each parcel, securing contents. Prepare sauce by mixing wasabi and soy.

To serve, place 2 sushi rolls on each plate with dipping sauce in a bowl or carefully slice rolls into thick widths and secure with a toothpick for pre-dinner nibbles.

Note   The moisture from the mayonnaise and salmon helps to secure the contents.

SMOKED SALMON AND HORSERADISH CREAM ROLLS

SERVES 2

prep time: 10 minutes

cook time: 2 minutes

4   **tablespoons light cottage and cream cheese blend**
2   **tablespoons *horseradish cream* (see page 167)**
4   **egg rolls (see page 30)**
4   **ounces smoked salmon, cut into ¾-inch slices**
2   **teaspoons lemon juice**
1   **tablespoon capers**
1   **handful baby spinach**

Mix cheese blend and horseradish cream. Place rolls on a cutting board and spread with cheese mixture. Evenly distribute salmon across each roll. Squeeze a little lemon juice on top and sprinkle with capers. Place a few spinach leaves over salmon and roll each parcel, securing contents. Serve rolls on a plate or carefully slice into thick widths and serve with drinks.

Note   This dish carries a little more fat than desired, so make it an occasional treat or for when you are simply maintaining your ideal weight. See picture of this dish between pages 26 and 27.

Variation   Use a tuna, ricotta and arugula combination with a squeeze of lemon juice as an alternative lower-fat filling.

LEMONGRASS AND GINGER CHICKEN BALLS

prep time: 10 minutes

cook time: 25 minutes

¾	**pound minced chicken breast**
1	**large handful mint, finely chopped**
1	**large handful cilantro, finely chopped**
1	**1½-inch piece ginger, finely chopped**
3	**whole spring onions, finely chopped**
1	**stalk celery, finely chopped**
1	**handful water chestnuts, finely chopped**
2	**stalks lemongrass, finely chopped (use white part only, usually the first 2–3 inches of stalk)**
2	**teaspoons sesame oil**
2	**teaspoons fish sauce**
2	**tablespoons sesame seeds**
	pickled ginger and soy dipping sauce **(see page 164) or light soy**

Preheat oven to 425°F. Combine all ingredients except sesame seeds and mix well. Roll mixture into balls, roughly the size of a golf ball, and place on a non-stick tray or tray lined with non-stick baking paper. Sprinkle the tops with sesame seeds and bake for 15–20 minutes or until cooked through. Then place under a hot grill for 5 minutes or until sesame seeds are golden. Serve on a large plate with dipping sauce in a bowl.

Note   Serve balls as a light lunch with a simple green salad, Chinese cabbage, shredded beet and cashews (see page 136) or watermelon and cucumber salsa (see page 171). Balls can be steamed instead of baked. For a serious shortcut, place all ingredients (except chicken) in a food processor until finely chopped and then combine with minced chicken. This will give a smoother texture. I prefer to put in the extra time to achieve a chunkier taste and look.

Variation   Reduce ball size and serve as pre-dinner nibbles.

PROSCIUTTO, FRESH FIG AND GOAT CHEESE

SERVES 4

prep time: 2 minutes

cook time: 2 minutes

2   slices prosciutto

2   fresh figs

1   tablespoon goat cheese marinated in oil or low-fat feta marinated in oil
       olive oil spray
       pure maple syrup (optional)

Preheat oven to 425°F or heat barbecue grill to high or place a non-stick griddle over high heat. Slice prosciutto in half lengthways and figs in half vertically. Spread a little goat cheese over each fig and wrap prosciutto around to form 4 small parcels. Lightly spray figs with oil and bake for 15 minutes or until prosciutto is golden and crisp. Drizzle with a little maple syrup and serve as a starter on a small bed of arugula or mixed lettuce, or as a side dish with chicken, pork or veal.

Note   These little packages are relatively low in carbohydrates, but they are high in saturated fat. If cooked on a grill, they will take only 2–3 minutes each side. See picture of this dish between pages 26 and 27.

Variation   Cut figs into bite-sized pieces, use a little more cheese and make mini parcels to serve with drinks as pre-dinner nibbles.

TUNA, CELERY AND LEMON DIP

MAKES 4 CUPS

prep time: 5 minutes

1	pound (16 ounces) canned tuna in oil, drained
6	ounces light cottage and cream cheese blend
4	ounces low-fat plain yogurt
3–4	tablespoons lemon juice
2	stalks celery, finely chopped
2	English cucumbers, finely chopped
	good pinch of sea salt

Combine tuna, cheese blend, yogurt and lemon juice in a bowl and mix well. Gently fold in celery and cucumber, being careful not to overblend. Add salt to taste.

Serve with cucumber, celery, green and red pepper sticks or cornichons and crispbreads. Dollop a tablespoon in a romaine, Belgian endive or iceberg leaf or fill a few celery stalks for a snack.

Variation   Add 2 teaspoons Dijon mustard to the recipe for extra bite.

🥀 *kid friendly*   Fussy little eaters will devour this dip, which was inspired by my Irish friend Ciara. Place a dollop in a bowl and stick a variety of vegetables in it – snow peas, beans, celery and baby carrots.

ROASTED BEET DIP

MAKES 4 CUPS

prep time: 5 minutes

cook time: 30 minutes

4	**beets (about 10–12 ounces)**
6	**ounces light cottage and cream cheese blend**
4	**ounces low-fat plain yogurt**
2	**tablespoons lime juice**
2	**handfuls mint (optional), freshly chopped**
	sea salt

Preheat oven to 425°F. Slice beets in half, place on foil squares and tightly wrap. Bake for 30 minutes or until cooked. A fork should go in quite easily. Remove from oven to a food processor. Blend or process all ingredients except mint. Fold mint through dip, season with salt to taste and serve or use as a spread on shaved turkey or lettuce for a snack. Serve with grilled or roasted chicken, lamb or beef.

Note   All dips are extremely versatile and work well with large numbers and barbecues. Beets are an excellent source of flavonoids – a powerful antioxidant found in many vegetables and fruit, particularly berries. As an antioxidant, it prevents oxidization in the body and fights free radicals. Beets are also rich in potassium, which helps to maintain nerve function and blood pressure, and are a good source of the vitamin folate or folic acid, deficiency of which may cause anemia, poor growth and depression. See picture of this dish between pages 26 and 27.

Variation   Add a small handful of chopped chives instead of mint and a garlic clove, and use low-fat ricotta instead of cheese blend.

LOW-CARB PIZZA

SERVES 2

prep time: 5 minutes

cook time: 7–10 minutes

2   **handfuls spinach, roughly chopped**

1   **cup canned tuna in oil, drained**

8   **kalamata olives, pitted and sliced**

2   **tablespoons capers**

6   **tablespoons grated low-fat mozzarella**

Low-Carb Pizza Base

2   **slices soft, flat bread**

4   **tablespoons *roasted tomato sauce* (see page 160)**

Preheat oven to 400°F. To assemble pizza base, cut each slice of bread into 3 equal slices. Place on a tray lined with baking paper. Spread tomato sauce over bread.

On each pizza slice, layer spinach, tuna, olives and capers, and sprinkle with mozzarella. Bake for 7–10 minutes or until cheese has melted and edges are crisp.

Note You will need to eat these pizzas with a knife and fork. The kids can simply roll them up.

Variations Try any of these topping combinations for quick, delicious snacks or lunches: prosciutto, arugula, bocconcini and basil or shaved light ham, button mushrooms, grated low-fat Cheddar cheese and Dijon mustard. (Spread 1 tablespoon mustard over soft, flat bread before adding tomato sauce.) Smoked salmon with finely sliced red onion and a few spinach leaves with some cottage and cream cheese blend is also delicious. The simpler the combination, the better.

🌸 *kid friendly* without capers or olives.

SWEET POTATO, MUSHROOM AND BASIL PIE

SERVES 4

prep time: 10 minutes

cook time: 35–40 minutes

4	**eggs**
2	**egg whites**
½	**cup grated sharp, aged Cheddar cheese (about 2 ounces)**
½	**cup grated mild Cheddar cheese (about 2 ounces)**
½	**cup light evaporated milk**
2	**handfuls basil, roughly chopped**
	sea salt
	cracked pepper
	olive oil/olive oil spray
5¼	**ounces sweet potato, finely sliced into 10 rounds**
2	**large mushrooms (about 8 ounces), sliced**
1	**tablespoon grated Parmesan**

Preheat oven to 350°F. Whisk eggs and egg whites and combine with cheeses, milk and basil. Season with salt and pepper. Spray or brush a non-stick, 10-inch-round baking dish with oil. Place a single layer of sweet potato on base and then place mushroom slices on top. Pour over egg mixture and sprinkle with Parmesan. Bake for 35–40 minutes or until golden on top and firm to touch.

To serve, slice into wedges and serve with a simple green salad. This recipe serves 2 for dinner.

Variations   Use about 1 cup pumpkin instead of sweet potato for a slightly lower-carbohydrate alternative, or double the mushrooms, lightly sauté them and forget the sweet potato for a very low-carb dish.

BROCCOLI, FETA AND ROASTED
RED PEPPER FRITTATA

SERVES 4

prep time: 10 minutes

cook time: 25–30 minutes

1	**red pepper**
4	**eggs**
2	**egg whites**
½	**cup light evaporated milk**
2	**tablespoons *basil pesto* (see page 162)**
	sea salt
	cracked pepper
1	**cup broccoli florets, chopped into small, bite-sized pieces**
	olive oil/olive oil spray
½	**cup low-fat feta**

Preheat broiler to high. Cut pepper in half lengthways. Remove seeds and pith. Place on a tray lined with parchment paper or non-stick tray and bake pepper cut-side down for 20 minutes or until black and blistered. Remove and place pepper in a plastic bag for 10 minutes. Then remove the skin and slice the pepper into long thin strips. Combine eggs, egg whites, milk, pesto, salt and pepper, and whisk. Add broccoli. Heat a non-stick, 10-inch frying pan with heatproof handle over medium heat and brush or spray with oil. Pour egg mixture into pan and reduce heat to low. Cook for 4–5 minutes or until frittata is almost set. Be careful not to burn or brown the bottom. Place pepper strips at random on frittata and crumble over feta. Lightly spray with olive oil and place under hot broiler for 2–3 minutes or until golden.

To serve, slice into wedges and serve with a simple green salad.

Note   Cook additional peppers and use for roasted red pepper sauce (see chapter 7), or add to omelets, salads or antipasto platters. A shortcut to roasting peppers is to place them directly on a gas burner or electric hotplate. This will give a smoked flavor and the pepper will be a little firmer but just as delicious. This recipe will serve 4 as a starter and 2 as a main meal with salad. See picture of this dish opposite page 42.

Variations   Instead of pesto, try 2 handfuls freshly chopped dill or basil. Use goat cheese marinated in oil instead of feta, or add 12 kalamata olives, pitted and cut in half horizontally. Serve frittata with roasted red pepper sauce or roasted tomato sauce (see chapter 7). All frittata dishes look great served with some wilted spinach placed over the top and a few slices of roasted red pepper.

ASPARAGUS, LEEK AND PANCETTA FRITTATA

SERVES 2

prep time: 15 minutes

cook time: 15 minutes

	olive oil/olive oil spray
1	**leek, white part only, finely sliced**
4	**eggs**
2	**egg whites**
½	**cup light evaporated milk**
½	**cup shredded light Cheddar cheese**
	pinch of sea salt
	cracked pepper
6	**thick asparagus spears or 10–12 thinner spears**
6	**slices pancetta, trimmed**
½	**cup shredded Parmesan**

Preheat grill to high. Heat a non-stick, 10-inch frying pan over medium heat. When hot, spray or brush well with oil and add leek. Cook for 3–4 minutes or until soft. Meanwhile mix eggs, egg whites, milk, Cheddar cheese, salt and pepper. Snap asparagus where it breaks naturally, discarding ends. Slice in half lengthwise if spears are thick. Pour egg mixture into pan with leek and reduce heat. Press a layer of pancetta into egg mixture and then arrange asparagus in a line alternating heads and ends. When frittata is almost set, 4–5 minutes, sprinkle with Parmesan. Place under hot grill for 2–3 minutes or until golden and cooked through.

To serve, slice into wedges and serve with a simple green salad.

Note   Beware of handles that are not ovenproof. This also makes a delicious light supper for 4.

Variation   Serve with tomato and bocconcini or arugula, pear and pan-toasted walnut salad (see page 133).

CURRY LAMB AND MINT IN ROASTED PEPPERS

SERVES 4

prep time: 10 minutes

cook time: 30 minutes

4	red peppers	1	pound lean ground lamb
1	tablespoon olive oil	14	ounces canned peeled, diced tomatoes
1	clove garlic, finely chopped	1	tablespoon tomato paste
1	tablespoon grated ginger	2	tablespoons pine nuts
½	teaspoon turmeric	2	handfuls mint, finely chopped
½	teaspoon cumin	1	teaspoon sea salt
1	teaspoon curry powder	1	cup green peas
1	red onion, finely chopped	8	tablespoons *cucumber and mint yogurt sauce* (see page 163)
1	zucchini, chopped into small cubes		
1	carrot, chopped into small cubes		

Preheat oven to 400°F. Slice peppers in half horizontally, remove pith and seeds and place cut-side up in a non-stick baking dish or baking dish lined with parchment paper. Bake for 10–15 minutes, then remove from oven.

Place a large saucepan over medium to high heat. When hot, add oil, garlic, ginger and spices. Cook for 1 minute, then add vegetables. Cook for 2–3 minutes or until vegetables have softened. Push vegetables to the side and add meat. Cook for 3–4 minutes or until brown. Add tomatoes, tomato paste, pine nuts and mint and stir. Reduce heat and simmer for 10–15 minutes. Spoon lamb and vegetable mixture into peppers, cover with foil and return to oven for 10 minutes.

To serve, place 2 halves on each plate and dollop with cucumber and mint yogurt sauce.

Note   Use low-fat tzatziki for a convenient alternative to the sauce.

Variations   Use 1 cup finely chopped beans instead of peas. Spoon lamb and vegetables onto a piece of soft flat bread, wrap, spray with a little olive oil and bake for 15–20 minutes or until bread is crisp and golden. This variation has a few extra carbohydrates without the benefits of the peppers' high vitamin C, beta carotene and bioflavonoid content, but it makes a delicious change.

OPEN STEAK SANDWICH

SERVES 2

prep time: 5 minutes

cook time: 6 minutes

1	**slice soft flat bread**
4	**minute steaks (about ¼ pound each) or beef tenderloin (about 1 pound for 2)**
	sea salt
	cracked pepper
	olive oil/olive oil spray
1	**handful arugula or spinach**
4	**teaspoons *horseradish cream* (see page 167)**

Preheat oven to 400°F. Cut soft flat bread into 4 equal squares and bake for 5 minutes or until crisp and golden. Meanwhile season steaks with salt and pepper. If using tenderloin, cut into $1/3$-inch slices. Heat a non-stick griddle or frying pan over high heat. When hot, brush or spray with oil and add steaks. Cook for 1 minute each side and remove from pan.

To serve, place a few arugula leaves over each piece of bread and a piece of steak on top. Dollop horseradish cream on top of each piece of steak. Serve for lunch or with salad for a light supper.

Note This flat bread will curl a little, which actually looks very effective and holds the arugula and meat nicely.

Variations Use your favorite mustard (no added sugar), eggplant mash or spicy red pepper chutney (see page 169) instead of horseradish cream. Use spinach instead of arugula or serve with bocconcini and tomato salad.

TOFU WITH ASPARAGUS, WATER CHESTNUTS AND GINGER

SERVES 2

prep time: 10 minutes

cook time: 10 minutes

8	ounces firm tofu
2	large handfuls fresh bean sprouts
1	tablespoon sesame seeds
	olive oil/olive oil spray or safflower oil
12	thick spears asparagus, ends trimmed
4	large green onions, finely sliced
½	red pepper, finely sliced
½	cup water chestnuts, cut into 3–4 slices

Orange, Ginger and Chile Dressing

¼	cup fresh orange juice
½	small red chile, seeded and finely chopped
1	tablespoon light soy
1	teaspoon sesame oil
1	tablespoon freshly grated ginger

Prepare dressing by combining all ingredients in a screw-top jar and shaking vigorously. Cut tofu into ³⁄₄-inch cubes, place in a bowl and cover with dressing. Marinate for at least 10 minutes, longer if possible. Cover bean sprouts with cold water and soak for at least 10 minutes. Place sesame seeds in a non-stick frying pan and dry toast for 30 seconds or until golden.

Heat a large non-stick wok or frying pan over medium heat, then spray or brush with olive oil. Remove tofu from dressing and place in wok. Cook for 2–3 minutes or until golden, tossing regularly. Remove from pan and place on paper towels. Wipe wok and return to medium heat. Again spray or brush well with oil and add asparagus, green onion and pepper. Cook for 1–2 minutes, tossing regularly. Return tofu to pan, add water chestnuts and drained bean sprouts. Add dressing and gently toss. Cook for 1–2 minutes or until tofu and vegetables are warmed through.

To serve, ladle into shallow pasta bowls and sprinkle with sesame seeds.

Note   Tofu is a fabulous source of nutrients; it's high in protein, calcium and magnesium and low in fat. Tofu has virtually no taste so marinating prior to cooking is a good idea. It is not as low in carbohydrates as meat, but on average has only 3g carb per serving size of 100g. If you have time, wrap kitchen paper around tofu and place a weight on top to remove excess liquid an hour prior to cooking or marinating.

Variation   Use green beans, topped and tailed, instead of asparagus.

Opposite: Broccoli, Feta and Roasted Red Pepper Frittata (page 38)
Overleaf: Rare Beef Tenderloin, Radicchio and Parmesan (page 69)

CRISPY TOFU WITH PESTO AND ROASTED TOMATO SAUCE

SERVES 2

prep time: 5 minutes

cook time: 5 minutes

8	ounces firm tofu
	olive oil/olive oil spray
1–2	tablespoons *basil pesto* (see page 162)
½	cup *roasted tomato sauce* (see page 160)
4	handfuls baby spinach
1	handful basil, finely chopped
2	tablespoons shredded Parmesan

Wrap tofu in paper towels and remove excess moisture by applying gentle pressure. Chop tofu into ³/₄-inch cubes. Heat a large non-stick wok or frying pan over medium to high heat. When hot, spray or brush with oil and add tofu. Cook for 3–4 minutes or until golden, tossing regularly. Add pesto and mix well. Add tomato sauce, spinach and basil and gently cook until spinach collapses.

To serve, spoon into shallow soup bowls and sprinkle with Parmesan.

Note   If purchasing bottled or pre-packaged pesto or tomato sauce, avoid those with added sugar and starch.

Variation   Toss tofu with eggplant, red peppers and olives (see page 143). Treat tofu as gnocchi's distant cousin and experiment with different sauces. Its texture lends itself to numerous dishes.

Previous page: Fresh Tomato Soup (page 47)
Opposite: Calamari, Peppers and Pickled Ginger (page 63)

SOUP

We tend to think of soups as colder weather fare, but because of their convenience and general

ease of preparation they should not be forgotten during the warmer months of the year. Most

often the taste of soup improves overnight, so give the flavor a chance to infuse if you have

time. Soups with a high-protein component, such as Moroccan lamb; chicken, spinach and

green onion; seafood; and miso with asparagus and tofu, are meals in themselves and require

no second course. They all contain a good dose of protein as well as a variety of delicious herbs

and spices and low-carbohydrate vegetables jam-packed with vitamins and minerals. If you are

following some of the lighter soups, such as fresh tomato or pear and parsnip, with a main meal

or dessert, bear in mind that you have already consumed a good dose of vegetables (therefore

carbohydrates), albeit low-carb ones. For the main meal, accompany the protein component with

a very low-carbohydrate side dish, such as a simple green salad or green vegetables.

The soups are stock-based, which means making your own or buying stock in liquid, powder

or cube form. Many commercial liquid stocks are very salty and need to be watered down a

little. Try them before you use them and adjust the salt content as desired. The flavors of the

minestrone, and the zucchini and cauliflower soup can be enhanced by adding a ham hock to

the stock and allowing it to simmer for an hour or more.

Several of the soups have intense colors, making them ideal to serve in shot glasses with

pre-dinner drinks for something different. Try the carrot, orange and ginger or the roasted red

pepper. The most important thing is to be flexible with these recipes. For example, I have a love

affair with Asian parsley – also known as cilantro – and use it whenever I can, but if you don't

share this passion, just reduce the quantity or try a different herb. Use and adapt these recipes

to suit your taste.

CAULIFLOWER AND JERUSALEM ARTICHOKE

SERVES 6

prep time: 10 minutes

cook time: 30 minutes

1	tablespoon olive oil
1	yellow onion, roughly chopped
½	ripe cauliflower, roughly chopped
8	Jerusalem artichokes, peeled and roughly chopped
6	cups chicken stock
2	tablespoons shredded low-fat Cheddar cheese
	cracked pepper
	sea salt

Heat a large saucepan over medium heat. When hot, add oil and onion and cook for 2 minutes or until softened. Add cauliflower and artichoke and toss well. Add stock and bring to the boil. Reduce heat and simmer for 30 minutes. Remove from heat and blend or process until smooth.

To serve, ladle into bowls and sprinkle with cheese and cracked pepper. Season to taste.

Variations   Use a whole cauliflower, forget the artichokes and add 2 tablespoons shredded Parmesan. Replace artichokes with about $^{3}/_{4}$-pound broccoli.

🌸 *kid friendly*

FRESH TOMATO

prep time: 15 minutes

cook time: 30 minutes

1	**tablespoon olive oil**
2	**cloves garlic, finely sliced**
1	**yellow onion, chopped**
2	**stalks celery, chopped**
1	**red pepper, chopped**
12	**ripe tomatoes, chopped, or 2½ pounds peeled, diced tomatoes**
3	**cups chicken stock**
1	**teaspoon capers (optional)**
1	**teaspoon sea salt**
2	**tablespoons light sour cream**
1	**tablespoon *basil pesto* (see page 162) (optional)**
	cracked pepper

Heat a large saucepan over medium heat. When hot, add oil and garlic and cook for a few seconds. Add onion, celery and pepper and cook for further 2 minutes. Add tomato, stock, capers and salt. Bring to the boil, then simmer for 30 minutes. Remove from heat. Blend or process until smooth. For a very fine texture, strain soup through a sieve.

To serve, ladle into soup bowls, add a teaspoon light sour cream and ½-teaspoon pesto to each bowl and season with salt and pepper.

Note Straining soup will give a much smoother texture if that is your preference, but remember it does remove extra fiber from the meal. See picture of this dish between pages 42 and 43.

Variations Roast the tomato, onion and garlic, then add to celery, stock, capers and salt or omit celery and capers and add 1 tablespoon pesto and a handful of shredded basil.

🌸 *kid friendly*

CARROT, ORANGE AND GINGER

SERVES 6

prep time: 10 minutes

cook time: 35 minutes

1	tablespoon olive oil
1	red onion, chopped
10	baby carrots or 2 large, roughly chopped
2	cups savoy cabbage, roughly chopped
3	cups chicken stock
14	ounces peeled, diced tomatoes
1	teaspoon freshly grated ginger
¼	cup fresh orange juice
2	teaspoons orange zest
1	handful cilantro (optional), roughly chopped

Heat a large saucepan over medium heat. When hot, add oil and onion and cook until softened. Add carrot and cabbage and cook for 3–4 minutes. Add stock, tomato and ginger, cover and bring to the boil. Reduce heat and simmer for 30 minutes. Add juice and orange zest to soup, reserving a little zest for garnish, then blend or process. Keep soup at a simmer and add cilantro 5 minutes prior to serving, again reserving a little for garnish.

To serve, ladle into bowls and sprinkle with remaining zest and cilantro.

Note   Carrots contain fiber and are an excellent source of beta carotene, which can be turned into vitamin A by the body when needed. Beta carotene is a powerful antioxidant, which can protect against signs of aging and assists in good health and general well-being. Carrots, while low in carbohydrates, have a high glycemic index.

Variation   Add ½-cup light coconut milk when adding cilantro.

PEAR AND PARSNIP

SERVES 6

prep time: 5 minutes

cook time: 35 minutes

1	tablespoon olive oil
1	leek, sliced
2	cups savoy cabbage, sliced
2	ripe pears, peeled and roughly chopped
4	small parsnips, roughly chopped
5	cups chicken stock
2	tablespoons shredded Parmesan
	sea salt
	cracked pepper

Heat a large saucepan over medium heat. When hot, add oil, leek and cabbage and cook for 3–4 minutes, stirring regularly. Add pear and parsnip and stir well. Add stock and bring to the boil. Reduce heat and simmer for 30 minutes. Remove from heat and blend or process. Season with salt and pepper.

To serve, ladle into soup bowls and sprinkle with Parmesan.

Note   Fi, a girlfriend of mine, makes a delicious pear and parsnip soup. With both pear and parsnip, the carbohydrate content is a little on the high side, but this version uses a few different ingredients to reduce the carbohydrate density and saturated fat.

ROASTED RED PEPPER WITH FETA

SERVES 6

prep time: 10 minutes

cook time: 30 minutes

6	red peppers
1	tablespoon olive oil
1	yellow onion, chopped
2	ripe tomatoes, chopped
2	cloves garlic, crushed
3	tablespoons tomato paste
4	cups chicken stock
¼	cup low-fat feta

Turn grill on high or heat oven to 425°F. Cut peppers in half lengthways and remove pith and seeds. Place cut-side down on a tray lined with parchment paper. Grill or bake for 20 minutes or until skin darkens and blisters. Remove peppers and place in a plastic bag for 10 minutes. Then peel and roughly chop. Heat a large saucepan over medium heat and add oil, onion, tomato and garlic. Cook for 2–3 minutes or until onion is soft. Add pepper to saucepan with tomato paste and stock. Bring to a boil then reduce heat and simmer for 10 minutes. Blend or process.

To serve, ladle into bowls and crumble feta on top.

Variations   Crumble goat cheese marinated in oil over the soup instead of feta, but remember that goat cheese is about 25-percent saturated fat. Instead of tomatoes, add an extra red pepper for a purer flavor.

LOW-CARB MINESTRONE WITH SHREDDED PARMESAN

SERVES 8

prep time: 10–15 minutes

cook time: 70 minutes

4	strips bacon		3	bay leaves
1	tablespoon olive oil		14	ounces peeled, diced tomatoes or
1	yellow onion, finely chopped			2 cups *roasted tomato sauce*
2	carrots, cut into thin slices			(see page 160)
2	stalks celery, finely chopped		½	cup dried split peas
¼	savoy or ½ Chinese cabbage, sliced,			cracked pepper
	or 8 brussels sprouts, quartered			sea salt
2	zucchini, cut into thin slices		2	handfuls parsley or cilantro,
1.5	quarts chicken stock			finely chopped
2	cloves garlic, crushed		4	tablespoons shredded Parmesan

Remove all visible fat from bacon and chop into $^3/_4$-inch squares. Heat a large saucepan over medium heat. When hot, add oil, onion and bacon. Cook for 2–3 minutes or until soft. Add vegetables to the saucepan. Gently stir and cook for about 5 minutes. Add stock, garlic, bay leaves, tomato and split peas. Increase heat and bring to the boil. Reduce heat and simmer, covered, for 1 hour. Season to taste.

Ladle into large bowls and sprinkle with parsley or cilantro and Parmesan.

Note   The flavor of this dish intensifies with further cooking – simmer for another hour with the lid on – and is even better the next day. This is a great soup for entertaining large numbers.

Variations   Add 2 tablespoons basil pesto or fresh basil instead of cilantro or parsley. For increased protein and carbohydrate add $^1/_2$-cup canned or cooked cannellini or soybeans or lentils or 1 pound firm tofu cut into small cubes. Use beef or vegetable stock instead of chicken stock.

SEAFOOD, TOMATO AND FLAT-LEAF PARSLEY

SERVES 4

prep time: 5 minutes

cook time: 30 minutes

1	tablespoon olive oil
6	cloves garlic, crushed
1	pound assorted seafood (see note)
3	cups fish stock
1	tablespoon fish sauce
14	ounces canned peeled, diced tomatoes
2	handfuls flat-leaf parsley, freshly chopped
	sea salt
	cracked pepper
2	tablespoons low-fat sour cream

Heat a large saucepan over medium heat. When hot, add oil and garlic and stir. Add seafood mix and cook for 1 minute. Add fish stock, fish sauce and tomato. Bring to the boil and reduce heat to simmer, covered, for 30 minutes. Add parsley. Season to taste.

To serve, ladle into warm bowls and drizzle with a little sour cream.

Note   For this soup recipe, choose a selection of your favorite seafood; prawns, scallops and calamari make a great combination or add some firm whitefish fillets, cut into bite-sized pieces.

Variation   Add some finely chopped chile for a kick.

CHICKEN, SPINACH AND GREEN ONION

SERVES 4

prep time: 10 minutes

cook time: 17 minutes

2	**handfuls bean sprouts**
2	**quarts chicken stock**
12	**green onions, finely sliced (discard last 2–4 inches)**
4	**chicken thigh fillets, cut into ¾-inch slices**
2	**tablespoons freshly grated ginger**
1	**carrot, shredded or cut into long, fine strips**
1	**teaspoon white miso paste (optional)**
2	**large handfuls spinach, roughly chopped**

Place bean sprouts in a bowl and soak in cold water for at least 10 minutes. Add chicken stock and green onion (reserving a little for garnish) to a large saucepan. Cover and bring to the boil, then reduce heat. Simmer, covered, for 10 minutes. Add chicken, ginger, carrot and miso. Cover and gently simmer until chicken is just cooked, about 5 minutes. Add spinach to soup with drained bean sprouts and cook for a further 1–2 minutes.

To serve, ladle into bowls and sprinkle with remaining green onion and cracked pepper.

Note   If using baby spinach in this recipe, do not chop.

Variations   Use pork fillets or add steamed lemongrass and ginger chicken balls (see page 32) instead of chicken fillet.

CHICKEN, BROCCOLINI, CHOY SUM AND COCONUT MILK

SERVES 4

prep time: 5 minutes

cook time: 10 minutes

1	(⅓-ounce) packet dashi powder
1	cup boiling water
2	cups chicken stock
2	stalks lemongrass, finely chopped (first 2–3 inches only)
1	tablespoon fish sauce
1	small fresh chile, seeded and finely chopped
6	skinless chicken thigh fillets
1	cup light coconut milk
2	cups broccolini, including stem, cut diagonally into bite-sized pieces
1	bunch choy sum, cut diagonally into bite-sized pieces
1	small handful cilantro or basil, freshly chopped

Mix dashi and boiling water and pour into a large saucepan over high heat. Add stock, lemongrass, fish sauce and chile. Bring to the boil, then cover. Remove any visible fat from chicken and slice into vertical $3/4$-inch strips. Add to boiling stock, then reduce heat and simmer. Add coconut milk and stir. Add broccolini and choy sum and simmer for 1–2 minutes.

To serve, ladle into large bowls and sprinkle with cilantro to taste.

Note   Use bok choy or spinach if choy sum is unavailable and use broccoli if broccolini is unavailable.

MOROCCAN LAMB

SERVES 6

prep time: 20 mins

cook time: 60–120 minutes

2	pounds lamb loin chops
	sea salt
	cracked pepper
	olive oil spray
2	yellow onions, finely chopped
4	stalks celery and leaves, finely chopped
2	quarts chicken stock
28	ounces peeled, diced tomatoes
½	cup red lentils
2	handfuls flat-leaf parsley, stalk and leaves, roughly chopped
2	handfuls cilantro, roughly chopped, or *cilantro, parsley and lemon salsa* (see page 172)

Moroccan Spices

1	teaspoon cumin
1	teaspoon turmeric
1	teaspoon paprika
1	teaspoon cinnamon

Trim all fat from lamb. Cut chops in half and season with salt and pepper. Heat a large saucepan over medium to high heat. When hot, spray well with oil and add lamb. Cook for 2 minutes on each side or until golden. Remove lamb and place on paper towels. Add onion and celery stalks and cook until soft, about 2 minutes. Add Moroccan spices and cook for a further minute. Add chicken stock, lamb, celery leaves, tomatoes, lentils and parsley. Bring to the boil, then reduce heat, cover and simmer for 1–2 hours.

To serve, ladle into bowls making sure each serving receives a piece of lamb. Sprinkle with cilantro or salsa and season to taste.

Note This is a delicious low-carb version of my friend Toni's recipe – a great dish for large numbers with a flavor that improves overnight. Once you've trimmed all visible fat from the lamb, there will still be some excess fat after cooking. If you have time, allow the soup to cool and then remove solidified fat. If you're eating the soup the same day and it is still warm, press a piece of plastic wrap over the top to remove most of the fat.

Variations Add ¹/₂-cup canned cannellini beans. If you prefer dried beans, soak them overnight and add to soup with chicken stock. The addition of lentils or cannellini beans will increase the carbohydrate content of this dish by 15–20g. If you are being vigilant about your carbs to get to your ideal weight, use split peas or 2 chopped carrots instead.

ZUCCHINI, CAULIFLOWER AND CRISPY PANCETTA

SERVES 4

prep time: 10–15 minutes

cook time: 35 minutes

1	tablespoon olive oil
1	yellow onion, roughly chopped
1	clove garlic, finely chopped
4	zucchini, roughly chopped
½	cauliflower, roughly chopped
4	cups chicken stock
2	tablespoons fresh dill
2	slices pancetta or prosciutto (optional)
2	tablespoons low-fat ricotta (optional)
	sea salt
	cracked pepper
2	tablespoons grated Parmesan

Heat oil in a large saucepan over medium heat. When hot, add onion and garlic. Cook for 2 minutes or until soft. Add zucchini and cauliflower and cook for a further 2 minutes. Add stock and dill. Cover and bring to the boil, then reduce heat and simmer for 30 minutes. Remove from heat and blend or process. Meanwhile, heat a griddle or non-stick frying pan over medium heat. Add pancetta and cook for 1 minute each side or until crisp. Remove and place on paper towels. Add ricotta to soup and stir well.

To serve, season with salt and pepper, and sprinkle over crumbled pancetta and Parmesan.

MISO WITH ASPARAGUS AND TOFU

SERVES 4

prep time: 5 minutes

cook time: 10 minutes

10	thick asparagus spears
2	tablespoons white miso paste
6	cups water
6	green onions, finely sliced
½	pound silken tofu, cut into ¾-inch cubes
1	tablespoon light soy
1	egg

Snap ends off asparagus where they break naturally and slice into 1¼-inch diagonals. Mix miso paste with a little boiling water. Add additional water to make up 6 cups and pour into a large saucepan. Add green onion, asparagus, tofu and soy. Cover and bring to the boil. Reduce heat and simmer for 3–4 minutes or until asparagus is just cooked. Meanwhile beat egg and slowly drizzle into soup with a fork, making thin egg noodles.

To serve, ladle into deep soup bowls.

Variation   Add some finely sliced nori (seaweed) to the dish before serving.

SALAD MAINS

A low-carb lifestyle embraces salads as a significant part of the daily diet. The salad as a

lunch or main course is a fabulous way to use the three food elements and different flavors

in combinations you would not ordinarily attempt if you were preparing a more standard meal

of meat and three vegetables. The varieties of salad leaves available, including arugula, leaf and

butter lettuce, radicchio and spinach through to endive, mizuna and watercress, together with

the many other vegetables, herbs, nuts, cheeses and dressings (see chapter 7), provide a

multitude of options. Add to the equation your major source of protein – fish, poultry or white

or red meat – plus low-carbohydrate fruit and vegetables and the possibilities are endless.

The recipes here range from hearty Thai beef to a light chicken slaw. Some involve a little work, others can be put together in minutes, such as the tuna, arugula and beets; the shaved turkey breast, apple and toasted walnuts; and the salmon, capers and dill on lettuce slices.

Salads have traditionally been enjoyed during the warmer months as the perfect companion to barbecues, but with a low-carb program fresh, fantastic salads are now important components of mealtimes all year round. Serve salads on individual plates or present them on a large platter, and mix colors, textures and shapes.

TUNA, ARUGULA AND BEETS

SERVES 4

prep time: 10 minutes

cook time: 5 minutes

8	baby beets, trimmed (leaving a ¾-inch stalk)
4	handfuls arugula
1	pound canned tuna in oil, drained
3	vine-ripened tomatoes, chopped into ¾-inch cubes, or 16 cherry tomatoes, halved
2	English cucumbers, chopped into ¾-inch cubes
½	red onion, finely sliced
2	tablespoons lemon juice or balsamic vinegar
1–2	tablespoon flaxseed oil or olive oil
	sea salt
	cracked pepper

Steam or microwave beets until just cooked, about 5 minutes. When cooked, slice into 4 segments.

To serve, place a handful of arugula on each plate and crumble tuna on top. Scatter tomatoes, beets, cucumber and red onion over tuna. Squeeze lemon, drizzle oil and season to taste.

Note   This salad and the salmon recipe on page 61 are two of the mainstays of my low-carbohydrate lifestyle. They are delicious, nutritious and prepared in minutes. You can find delicious pre-cooked baby beets in most supermarkets. If preparing your own beans (see below), soak them overnight and cook in chicken stock. Freeze excess in 1-cup quantities.

Variations   Replace arugula with baby spinach or finely shredded Chinese cabbage; add ½-cup cooked cannellini, Great Northern or soybeans. These beans or legumes will increase the carbohydrate density, nutritional value and fiber content of the dish. Add 2 large handfuls baby green beans, topped and lightly steamed, or a little ricotta or low-fat tzatziki. Crumbled feta or marinated goat cheese is also excellent with this salad, but remember goat cheese has 25-percent saturated fat.

kid friendly without baby beets.

SALMON, CAPERS AND DILL ON LETTUCE SLICES

SERVES 4

prep time: 5 minutes

cook time: 5 minutes

4	**eggs**
1	**avocado, diced**
½	**English cucumber, peeled and diced**
1	**handful fresh dill, finely chopped**
½	**head, iceberg lettuce**
1	**pound canned pink salmon, drained**
16	**tablespoons cottage cheese**
¼	**red onion, finely chopped**
1	**tablespoon capers**

Place eggs in a saucepan with enough water to cover and boil for 5 minutes. Leave to cool in cold water. Gently mix avocado, cucumber and half the dill. Peel eggs and finely chop. Cut lettuce vertically into $^3/_4$-inch slices.

To serve, place 8 lettuce slices onto a large platter. Spoon 2 tablespoons cottage cheese onto each slice and place salmon on top. Add avocado mixture and sprinkle each slice with a little chopped onion, egg, capers and remaining dill.

Note   By removing the bones from the salmon you are losing an excellent source of calcium and texture. If your skin and nails are looking a little dull and your hair is flat, a lower-carbohydrate lifestyle with increased lean protein and decreased saturated fat will help. This salad of salmon and egg has a good dose of sulfur, known as the "beauty" mineral.

Variations   Use fresh pan-seared salmon, canned tuna or mackerel. Use baby romaine leaves, instead of sliced iceberg lettuce.

SMOKED TROUT, AVOCADO AND WATERCRESS

prep time: 5 minutes

2	green onions, finely sliced diagonally
1	avocado, finely sliced
4	vine-ripened tomatoes, chopped into ¾-inch cubes
2	sun-dried tomatoes, finely sliced
2	handfuls watercress, large stalks removed
2	handfuls spinach
1	handful fresh dill, roughly chopped
½	pound smoked trout
3	tablespoons lemon juice
1	tablespoon flaxseed oil or extra virgin olive oil
	sea salt
	cracked pepper

Place green onion, avocado, tomato, watercress, spinach and dill in a shallow bowl. Tear smoked trout into small pieces and add to salad. Pour over lemon juice and oil, sprinkle with salt and pepper and toss well.

To serve, spoon into deep bowls.

Note   This salad is much lower in protein than other salads and main meals, so include it only occasionally in your low-carb lifestyle.

Variations   Use arugula or green oakleaf lettuce to replace watercress and/or spinach. Use a little dill and mustard sauce (see page 163) to replace lemon juice and flaxseed oil. Use smoked mackerel or salmon instead of trout.

CALAMARI, PEPPERS AND PICKLED GINGER

SERVES 4

prep time: 5 minutes

cook time: 5 minutes

2	tablespoons sesame seeds or poppyseeds
14	ounces calamari
	sea salt
1	tablespoon peanut oil
2	teaspoons sesame oil
½	red onion, finely sliced into wedges
1	red pepper, cut into long, thin strips
1	green pepper, cut into long, thin strips
4	large handfuls mixed greens
½	English cucumber, cut into long, thin strips
1	handful mint, finely chopped or roughly torn
4	tablespoons lime juice
2	tablespoons fish sauce
2	tablespoons pickled ginger

Preheat oven to 425°F. Place sesame seeds on a non-stick baking tray or tray lined with parchment paper and bake for 5 minutes or until golden. Clean, dry and score calamari with a sharp knife (to make small diamond shapes). Cut into 1 x 2-inch pieces and sprinkle with a little salt. Heat a non-stick griddle or frying pan over high heat. When hot, add peanut oil and sauté calamari for 1 minute or until golden and tender. Remove onto paper towels. Add 1 tablespoon sesame oil to pan, then add onion and peppers. Sauté for 1–2 minutes, then remove from heat. Combine all ingredients on a large platter. Scatter with seeds, drizzle with lime juice, fish sauce, pickled ginger and remaining sesame oil and toss well.

Serve from platter at the table.

Note   Poppyseeds do not need to be baked. See picture of this dish opposite page 43.

Variations   Use cuttlefish instead of calamari or fresh ginger instead of pickled. Add a handful of cilantro and/or basil, and for some extra heat, add some finely chopped chile or a little chile powder to the salt.

MOROCCAN CHICKEN WITH MARINATED FETA

prep time: 10 minutes

cook time: 5 minutes

2	skinless chicken breast fillets
1	tablespoon crushed cashews or slivered almonds
	olive oil/olive oil spray
¼	red onion, finely sliced
1	stalk celery, finely sliced into diagonals
1	red pepper, sliced into thin strips
1	handful mint, roughly torn
3	handfuls green oakleaf, leaf or butter lettuce
3	tablespoons marinated low-fat feta

Moroccan Spices

1	tablespoon powdered ginger
1	tablespoon cumin
1	tablespoon paprika
1	tablespoon turmeric
1	teaspoon cinnamon

Yogurt Dressing

2	tablespoons low-fat plain yogurt
2	tablespoons whole egg mayonnaise
1	tablespoon lemon juice

Cut each chicken breast lengthwise into 3 pieces. Combine Moroccan spices and sprinkle lightly over chicken strips. Heat a large non-stick griddle or frying pan over medium to high heat. Add cashews and dry roast for 2–3 minutes. Remove and set aside. Lightly spray or brush chicken with oil. When griddle is hot add chicken. Cook for 2 minutes on each side or until cooked through. Slice chicken pieces diagonally into $^3/_4$-inch widths. Combine yogurt, mayonnaise and lemon. Combine chicken, onion, celery, red pepper, mint and dressing and gently toss.

To serve, place a handful of salad mix on each plate. Place chicken mixture on top and crumble over feta.

Note This quantity of Moroccan spices will make enough for several salads or dishes. Place remaining Moroccan spices in an airtight container. Alternatively, excellent pre-packaged spice mixes can be purchased at most supermarkets and delicatessens, but beware of added sugar and starch.

Variations Use goat cheese marinated in oil instead of feta. Add $^1/_2$ avocado or $^1/_2$ ripe peach sliced into wedges. This recipe is also delicious with a cup of roasted sweet potato or pumpkin cut into $^3/_4$-inch cubes (a higher-carb option). Roll the chicken in *dukka* – a mild blend of Middle Eastern spices and nuts – instead of Moroccan spices and forget the cashews.

STEAMED CHICKEN SLAW WITH CHINESE SOY AND SESAME DRESSING

SERVES 4

prep time: 20–30 minutes

cook time: 10 minutes

1	handful bean sprouts
2	tablespoons sesame seeds or slivered almonds
4	skinless chicken breast fillets
2	handfuls cilantro, finely chopped
2	handfuls Vietnamese mint (or peppermint), finely sliced
¼	Chinese cabbage, finely sliced
1	red pepper, finely sliced into strips
4	green onions, finely sliced into diagonals
2	tablespoons fried shallots (optional)
6–8	tablespoons *Chinese soy and sesame dressing* (see page 165)

Heat oven to 425°F. Place bean sprouts in a bowl and soak in cold water for at least 10 minutes. Place sesame seeds on a non-stick baking tray or tray lined with parchment paper and bake for 5 minutes or until golden. Cut chicken in half vertically and steam or poach over medium heat for 7–10 minutes or until cooked. Remove chicken and allow to cool slightly. Shred chicken and add cilantro, half the mint, cabbage, red pepper, green onion, sesame seeds and drained bean sprouts to a large bowl. Add dressing and mix well.

To serve, place salad on a large platter and sprinkle with remaining mint and shallots.

Note   Dress this salad 1 hour before serving to intensify the flavor. Vietnamese mint is very hot so use ordinary mint if heat worries you. Fried shallots are loaded with saturated fat so don't overindulge – but a sprinkle tastes and looks so good.

Variations   Add a handful of chopped water chestnuts or shredded Jerusalem artichokes and/or a shredded carrot or 2 celery stalks finely sliced into diagonals. Add a handful of shredded red cabbage or beets, or a combination of both. Use snow pea sprouts instead of bean sprouts.

CHARGRILLED CHICKEN, CRISPY PROSCIUTTO AND BABY ROMAINE

SERVES 4

prep time: 10 minutes

cook time: 15 minutes

4	**skinless chicken breast fillets**
	sea salt
	cracked pepper
	olive oil/olive oil spray
4	**slices prosciutto**
6	**anchovy fillets (optional), drained**
2	**baby romaine**
1	**pint cherry tomatoes, halved**
1	**tablespoon baby capers**
4	**tablespoons shredded Parmesan**
3–4	**tablespoons *lemon Caesar dressing* (see page 165)**

Slice chicken lengthwise into 3 thick strips. Season with salt and pepper. Heat a non-stick griddle or non-stick frying pan over medium heat. Lightly brush or spray chicken with oil. When griddle is hot, add chicken and cook for 3–5 minutes each side or until golden. Remove onto paper towels. Slice chicken into $3/4$-inch diagonals. Reheat griddle over medium heat and add prosciutto. Cook for 2–3 minutes or until crisp. Tear prosciutto into long pieces. Slice anchovy fillets into thin strips and roll on paper towels to remove excess oil.

To serve, stack romaine leaves on each plate. Pile chicken strips in the center and scatter over tomatoes, prosciutto, anchovy fillets, capers and Parmesan. Drizzle dressing over each serving.

Note   As a quick time-saver purchase a rotisserie chicken, remove the skin and use the lean breast meat. See picture of this dish opposite page 75.

Variations   Use as a side salad or starter by replacing chicken with 4 poached eggs. For a quick alternative dressing, combine 3 tablespoons commercial Caesar dressing (see chapter 9), 1 tablespoon lemon juice and 1 tablespoon white wine vinegar.

kid friendly by removing anchovy fillets and capers.

SHAVED TURKEY BREAST, APPLE AND TOASTED WALNUTS

SERVES 2

prep time: 10 minutes

cook time: 5 minutes

2   **teaspoons butter**

2   **tablespoons walnuts (shelled), roughly chopped**

     sea salt

2   **teaspoons grated Parmesan**

     lemon juice

2   **handfuls green leaf lettuce**

1   **green apple, finely sliced into segments**

1   **stalk celery, finely chopped**

1   **handful mint, roughly torn**

7   **ounces shaved turkey breast, torn into pieces**

     cracked pepper

Yogurt Dressing

2   **tablespoons low-fat plain yogurt**

1   **tablespoon whole egg mayonnaise**

1   **tablespoon lemon juice**

Heat a non-stick frying pan over medium heat. When hot, add butter and walnuts. Cook for 3–4 minutes, shaking regularly. Remove from heat, then sprinkle over salt and Parmesan. Squeeze a little lemon juice over apple (to stop discoloring). Place green leaf lettuce, apple, celery and mint in a large bowl. Combine yogurt, mayonnaise and lemon juice. Add turkey and dressing to salad and toss well.

To serve, pile salad high on each plate and sprinkle with walnut pieces. Season to taste.

Variations   Use butter lettuce or finely sliced Chinese cabbage instead of leaf lettuce. Replace apple with pear or, for a higher-carbohydrate alternative, use sliced mango. Substitute 2 small smoked chicken breasts for turkey but remember to remove the skin.

🌸 *kid friendly*

RARE BEEF TENDERLOIN, RADICCHIO AND PARMESAN

SERVES 4

prep time: 15 minutes

cook time: 20 minutes

	sea salt
	cracked pepper
1	**pound beef tenderloin**
2	**handfuls radicchio**
2	**handfuls spinach**
2	**tablespoons capers**
1	**pint cherry tomatoes, halved**
4	**tablespoons shaved Parmesan**
12	**kalamata or Ligurian olives, pitted and halved**
2	**tablespoons extra virgin olive oil**
1	**tablespoon lemon juice**

Preheat oven to 400°F. Sprinkle a little salt and pepper on a board and roll beef firmly across seasoning. Heat barbecue grill to high or place a griddle pan over high heat. Add beef and sear for 3 minutes each side or until beef has a golden crust. Remove and bake in oven for 10–15 minutes or longer, according to taste. Remove from oven and let rest for 10–15 minutes. Meanwhile, place radicchio and spinach on a large platter. Rinse capers and pat dry on paper towels.

To serve, finely slice fillet and mix with radicchio and spinach. Scatter over tomatoes, Parmesan, capers and olives. Drizzle with olive oil and lemon juice and season to taste.

Note   This is a great dish for entertaining larger numbers. For a cheaper alternative, use rib-eye or porterhouse. The meat should be cooked medium rare. See picture of this dish between pages 42 and 43.

Variations   Use arugula instead of radicchio and add 8 finely sliced radishes. Roll beef in crushed coriander seeds (see page 70) or sprinkle with herb salt (see page 176). Add 16 thin asparagus spears, snapped at the base and lightly steamed. Use crumbled dried olives instead of kalamata.

SERVES 4

prep time: 20 minutes

cook time: 20 minutes

3	**tablespoons coriander seeds**
1	**teaspoon sea salt**
1	**teaspoon cracked pepper**
1	**pound beef tenderloin**
	olive oil/olive oil spray
2	**tablespoons cashews, lightly crushed, or sesame seeds**
2	**green onions or ½ red onion, finely sliced**
2	**English cucumbers**
1	**red pepper**
4	**handfuls arugula**
2	**handfuls cilantro, chopped into 2-inch lengths**
2	**handfuls mint or Vietnamese mint, torn**
1	**red chile, seeded and finely chopped**
6–8	**tablespoons *Thai lime dressing* (see page 164)**

Preheat oven to 400°F. Finely crush coriander seeds, salt and pepper and spread mixture on a board. Roll beef firmly across seasoning. Heat a cast-iron frying or griddle pan over high heat. When hot, brush or spray with olive oil and add beef. Cook for 3 minutes each side or until golden crust forms. Remove from heat and place on a tray lined with parchment paper. Bake for 10–15 minutes until medium rare or longer, according to taste. Remove beef and let stand for 10–15 minutes. Place cashews on a tray lined with parchment paper. Bake for 10 minutes or until golden. Cut green onion in half lengthwise and chop into 2-inch lengths. Cut cucumber and red pepper in half lengthwise and then into thin strips.

To serve, mix arugula, green onion, cucumber, red pepper, herbs and chile on a large platter. Finely slice beef and add to salad. Drizzle with dressing and mix well. Sprinkle with roasted cashews.

Note   Beef can be cooked the day before and refrigerated – this actually makes it easier to slice finely.

Variations   Use chicken thigh fillets or lamb tenderloin instead of beef but adjust the cooking time. The lamb may need to bake for only 5 minutes, depending on the width of the tenderloin. Shredded beets, bean sprouts, finely sliced Chinese cabbage and celery in any combination can replace the arugula.

TANDOORI LAMB AND CRISPY EGGPLANT

SERVES 4

prep time: 20 minutes

cook time: 35 minutes

2	**tablespoons tandoori paste**
4	**tablespoons low-fat plain yogurt**
1	**pound boneless lamb loin chops**
1	**eggplant**
	olive oil/olive oil spray
	sea salt
2	**tablespoons pine nuts**
4	**handfuls butter, leaf or green oakleaf lettuce (about 7 ounces)**
4	**vine-ripened or roma tomatoes, finely sliced into segments**
	cracked pepper
8	**tablespoons *cucumber and mint yogurt sauce* (see page 163)**

Preheat oven to 425°F. Combine tandoori paste with yogurt. Marinate lamb for at least 15 minutes, or overnight if possible. Meanwhile slice eggplant vertically into $1/3$-inch slices and each slice into 4 wedges. Place on a tray lined with parchment paper, spray with oil and sprinkle with salt. Bake for 20–25 minutes or until golden. Place pine nuts on a non-stick tray and bake for 5–10 minutes or until golden. Heat a large griddle or frying pan over medium to high heat or heat barbecue grill to high. When hot, spray or brush pan with oil and add lamb. Cook for 3–5 minutes on each side or until medium rare. Remove and rest for 10 minutes.

To serve, combine lettuce, tomato and eggplant on a large plate. Finely slice lamb and scatter over salad. Drizzle dressing over meat and scatter with pine nuts. Season with cracked pepper and sea salt.

Variations Use chicken thigh fillets, trimmed of fat and sliced vertically into 3 pieces. Low-fat tzatziki is a convenient and delicious alternative for the dressing. Just add $1/2$ English cucumber finely chopped and a handful of chopped mint to the salad.

MEATY MAINS

During my "low-fat" days I avoided meat because of its relatively high levels of saturated fat

and its detrimental effect on cholesterol levels. Now, however, as pasta and rice are no longer

options for the basis of my main meal, my focus has moved towards lean protein, preferably low

in saturated fats and high in vitamins and minerals. Today the levels of saturated fat have been

greatly reduced with the many new lean cuts of meat available.

There are hundreds of different cuts available of chicken, turkey, beef, veal, lamb and

pork and with the many varieties of fish and shellfish you could eat a different protein

source every day for months. All meat dishes in this chapter are trimmed of any visible

fat and minimal oil is added during the cooking process. Where possible the meat is

baked, barbecued, seared or grilled on a griddle pan and where appropriate placed on

paper towels to absorb excess fat. Cooking methods vary significantly depending on the

meat used.

There are slow-baking dishes such as lamb shank with cauliflower mash, Moroccan chicken with pumpkin and cilantro, and beef and mushroom in red wine. These dishes, while taking a little longer to cook, are simple and quick to prepare and their flavor infuses overnight. These rustic meals are great "comfort" dishes for the colder months and are also fabulous for entertaining, served with a simple salad. There is a large selection of quick-prep meals that are cooked in minutes, ranging from stirfries, such as the pork and lime with eggplant and red pepper, to stacks with veal, turkey or chicken. If fish is something you've personally avoided cooking, then read these simple delicious recipes. Many dishes are influenced by different ethnic cuisines with a strong focus on herbs and spices. Marinating meat prior to cooking is another healthy, wonderful and tasty way to increase flavor. Generally, the longer the marinating time, the better. You'll find plenty of ideas here for dinner parties or simple meals for two, so consider the wonderful health benefits of protein-based meals and start cooking.

CHARGRILLED TUNA, GREEN BEANS AND CHERRY TOMATOES

SERVES 4

prep time: 10 minutes

cook time: 10 minutes

4	tuna steaks (about 8 ounces each)
	olive oil/olive oil spray
	sea salt
6	anchovy fillets (optional)
1	pound green beans, trimmed
1	pint cherry tomatoes, halved
12	kalamata olives, roughly split and pitted
1	tablespoon baby capers
2	tablespoons lemon juice
4	handfuls arugula or spinach
	cracked pepper

Spray or lightly brush fish with oil, sprinkle with salt and let stand. Place anchovy fillets on paper towels, press to remove excess oil and roughly chop. Heat a large non-stick griddle pan over medium to high heat. When hot, lightly brush or spray with oil and add tuna. Cook for 2–3 minutes each side until medium rare, or longer according to taste. Remove from pan and keep warm. Add a little more oil to pan and increase heat. Add beans and sauté for 1–2 minutes. Add tomatoes, olives, capers and anchovies and sauté for a further minute. Add lemon juice, stir and remove from heat immediately.

To serve, place a handful of arugula on each plate with tuna on top. Scatter beans and tomatoes around. Ladle olives, capers and lemon juice over tuna and season to taste.

Note   Leave the slightly curved end (the tail) of the bean – it looks a lot better and means less work! You may want to lightly steam beans prior to sautéing. See picture of this dish opposite.

Variations   Salmon works just as well in this recipe or use drained, canned tuna in oil for a quicker version. Add $1/4$-cup cooked cannellini or soybeans or French green lentils to the pan at the same time as green beans, for a slightly higher-carbohydrate meal.

WASABI TUNA STEAKS WITH ZUCCHINI AND RED PEPPER

SERVES 4

prep time: 15 minutes

cook time: 10 minutes

4	tuna steaks (about 8 ounces each)
2	zucchini
2	carrots
1	red pepper
	sesame oil

Lemon and Wasabi Marinade

1	tablespoon freshly grated ginger
1	teaspoon wasabi
3	tablespoons light soy sauce
3	tablespoons lemon juice
2	tablespoons finely chopped cilantro (optional)
2	green onions, finely chopped (optional)

Combine marinade ingredients in a jar and shake well. Marinate tuna for at least 15 minutes and up to 1 hour. Slice zucchini, carrots and red pepper into long diagonals, then slice each piece into 3 chunky batons. Heat a non-stick frying pan over medium to high heat and when hot, brush with a little oil. Add tuna, retaining marinade, and cook for 2–3 minutes each side until medium rare, or longer according to taste. Meanwhile, heat a non-stick wok or frying pan over medium to high heat. When hot, brush with a little oil. Add vegetables and stirfry over high heat for 2–3 minutes, shaking constantly. Take off heat and add half the marinade. Shake vigorously, combining marinade and vegetables.

To serve, arrange vegetables in the center of each plate and position tuna on top. Shake remaining marinade vigorously and drizzle over tuna.

Variations Use salmon or any firm whitefish instead of tuna. Replace zucchini and carrots with a yellow or green pepper and 4 handfuls of round green beans, topped. For a completely different method, bake fish in individual parcels. Divide vegetables into 4 and place in the middle of a parchment-paper square (you will need 4 squares), then place tuna on top and drizzle with marinade. Tightly secure each parcel and bake at 400°F for 20 minutes for medium rare, or longer according to taste.

Opposite: Chargrilled Chicken, Crispy Prosciutto and Baby Romaine (page 67)

SESAME TUNA WITH WOK-TOSSED ASPARAGUS AND WATER CHESTNUTS

SERVES 4

prep time: 10 minutes

cook time: 10 minutes

1	handful bean sprouts
8	thick asparagus spears
2	tuna steaks (about 8 ounces each)
	olive oil/olive oil spray
1	tablespoon sesame seeds
1	red pepper, sliced into $\frac{1}{3}$-inch strips
$\frac{1}{2}$	cup water chestnuts, quartered

Orange, Ginger and Chile Marinade

$\frac{1}{4}$	cup freshly squeezed orange juice
$\frac{1}{2}$	small red chile, seeded and finely chopped
1	tablespoon light soy
1	tablespoon freshly grated ginger
1	teaspoon sesame oil

Place bean sprouts in a large bowl, cover with cold water and allow to soak. Place all marinade ingredients in a jar and shake well. Snap ends off asparagus where they break naturally and cut diagonally into thirds. Lightly spray or brush tuna with oil and sprinkle with sesame seeds. Heat a large non-stick frying pan over medium to high heat and when hot, lightly spray or brush with oil. Add tuna and cook for 2–3 minutes each side until medium rare, or longer according to taste. Meanwhile, place another non-stick wok or frying pan over medium to high heat. When hot, brush or spray with olive oil and add asparagus. Cook for 1 minute, shaking regularly. Add red pepper and cook for a further minute. Drain bean sprouts and add with water chestnuts to wok. Pour marinade over vegetables and toss well.

To serve, ladle vegetables into large shallow soup bowls or pasta plates, place tuna on top and drizzle with remaining marinade.

Variations   Use salmon instead of tuna and try green beans, snow peas or sugar snaps topped, not tailed, when asparagus is unavailable.

CAJUN SALMON WITH TOMATO, MANGO AND AVOCADO WEDGES

SERVES 4

prep time: 15 minutes

cook time: 5 minutes

4	salmon fillets (about 8 ounces each)
	olive oil/olive oil spray
2	roma tomatoes, cut into wedges
½	mango, cut into long slices
1	avocado, cut into long slices
¼	red onion (optional), cut into long slices
16	baby romaine leaves
8	tablespoons low-fat tzatziki

Cajun Spices

1	tablespoon onion powder
2	cloves garlic, crushed
2	teaspoons cracked pepper
2	teaspoons cayenne
1	tablespoon paprika
1	tablespoon oregano

Mix Cajun spices and sprinkle over salmon. Heat a large non-stick frying pan over medium to high heat. When hot, brush or spray with olive oil. Add salmon and cook for 2–3 minutes each side until medium rare, or longer according to taste. Gently mix tomato, mango, avocado and onion.

To serve, place romaine leaves on each plate, scatter over fruit and vegetables and place salmon on top. Dollop tzatziki on top of fish.

Note Excellent pre-packaged spices can be purchased from supermarkets and delicatessens, but look out for added sugar, starch and salt. The Cajun spices recommended here are quite hot so use sparingly. If you don't like too much heat, use a little salt and pepper instead or a mixture of fresh mint, parsley and onion powder.

Variations Use tuna or mackerel steaks instead of salmon. For a different flavor, roll salmon in *dukka* instead of Cajun spices. If you have time, make the cucumber and mint yogurt sauce (see page 163) and use instead of low-fat tzatziki.

BAKED SALMON IN BALSAMIC AND MAPLE SYRUP WITH SHAVED FENNEL

SERVES 2

prep time: 5 minutes

cook time: 20 minutes

1	**tablespoon olive oil**
1	**tablespoon balsamic vinegar**
2	**teaspoons maple syrup**
2	**salmon fillets (about 8 ounces each)**
1	**small fennel bulb, shredded**
½	**red onion, finely sliced**
1	**carrot, shredded**
1	**handful dill, finely chopped**
	olive oil/olive oil spray
	***parsnip chips* (see page 151, variation of *herb-salted turnip chips*)**

Preheat oven to 400°F. Combine oil, balsamic and maple syrup. Place salmon in marinade. Tear 2 large squares of parchment paper (about 1 foot each). Mix vegetables and dill and evenly distribute on the center of each square. Spray or brush vegetables with oil. Place salmon over the vegetables and drizzle remaining marinade on top. Tightly seal each package and place on a tray lined with parchment paper. Bake for 20 minutes for medium rare, or longer according to taste.

To serve, carefully remove fish and place vegetables on each plate. Arrange salmon over the vegetables and drizzle remaining marinade on top or simply place whole package on plate. Place parsnip chips in a pile alongside.

Note   Parsnip chips will take about 10–20 minutes, depending on their thickness, so time the baking of the salmon accordingly. See picture of this dish opposite page 107.

Variation   Use snow peas or celery instead of fennel, sliced into fine julienne, or substitute turnip or celeriac chips for parsnip chips for a lower-carbohydrate alternative.

CRISPY SALMON WITH PEPPERS AND THAI LIME DRESSING

SERVES 4

prep time: 15 minutes

cook time: 10 minutes

4	salmon fillets (about 8 ounces each)
	olive oil/olive oil spray
	sea salt
20	thin asparagus spears
1	red onion, finely chopped into wedges, retaining base
1	red pepper, finely sliced into thin strips
1	green pepper, finely sliced into thin strips
1	large handful cilantro
4	handfuls arugula
	Thai lime dressing (see page 164)

Spray or lightly brush fish with oil and sprinkle with a little salt and let stand. Snap ends off asparagus where they break naturally and cut diagonally into thirds. Heat a large wok or non-stick frying pan over medium to high heat. When hot, spray or brush with oil and add fillets. Cook for 2–3 minutes each side for medium rare, or longer according to taste. Remove from wok and keep warm. Spray or brush wok with a little more oil, increase heat and add onion. Cook for 1 minute or until slightly softened. Add pepper and asparagus and sauté for a further 2 minutes. Add half the dressing and toss. Remove from wok. Add cilantro and arugula to wok with remaining dressing. Toss well.

To serve, place cilantro and arugula on each plate with vegetables on top. Place salmon on top of vegetables and drizzle with dressing.

Note   You can retain the cilantro roots, which have a wonderfully intense flavor. Simply peel and finely chop them and add to dressings or stirfries.

Variation   Use spinach instead of arugula or a combination of both. If you can't find asparagus, use about 8 ounces long or green beans with tops trimmed and cut into 2-inch pieces.

STEAMED GINGER SNAPPER WITH BABY BOK CHOY

SERVES 2

prep time: 10 minutes

cook time: 10–15 minutes

4	cups chicken stock
4	green onions, finely sliced diagonally
2	stalks celery, finely sliced into 2-inch strips
1	large carrot, finely sliced into 2-inch strips
2	cloves garlic, finely chopped
1–2	tablespoons grated ginger
1	whole baby snapper (about 1 pound)
4	baby bok choy
1	handful cilantro (optional)
½	lemon, cut into wedges

Pour stock into a large saucepan with a steamer and add green onion, celery, carrot, garlic and ginger to stock. Bring to the boil. Reduce heat, place fish in steamer and ladle some of the stock over fish. Steam for 10 minutes or until cooked. Remove fish from steamer and keep warm. Bring stock to the boil and add bok choy and cilantro. Cook for 1–2 minutes.

To serve, place fish on a platter and arrange bok choy, celery and carrot around fish. Ladle over just enough hot stock to moisten the dish. Serve in shallow pasta bowls, with lemon on the side.

Note   This stock is delicious and makes a wonderful soup for lunch the next day. Ginger is the key ingredient. Start with 1 tablespoon and if the flavor is not strong enough for you, add a little more. Ginger is an extremely powerful spice with excellent medicinal properties – it is said to raise the body's temperature (which improves circulation), fight infection, cure nausea and colds and help with depression. If using a commercial stock, check the salt content. You may wish to dilute stock: 3 cups stock to 1 cup water.

Variations   Use spinach or choy sum instead of bok choy, and add 1 tablespoon chopped and crushed lemongrass to the stock. For a different fish taste, use bream or carp instead of snapper.

🌸 kid friendly served with a little whole egg mayonnaise and parsnip and sweet potato chips. The fish is moist and delicate.

ORANGE ROUGHY, PICKLED GINGER AND ORANGE

SERVES 2

prep time: 15 minutes

cook time: 10 minutes

⅔   **cup orange juice (about 2 oranges freshly squeezed)**

1   **tablespoon pickled ginger, finely sliced**

¼   **teaspoon wasabi**

1   **pound orange roughy fillets**

4   **handfuls baby spinach**

    olive oil/olive oil spray

    ***watermelon and cucumber salsa* (see page 171)**

Mix juice, ginger and wasabi. Place fish in marinade. Heat a large non-stick frying pan over medium to high heat. When hot, spray or brush with oil and add fish, retaining marinade. Cook for 3–4 minutes each side or until just cooked. Remove and keep warm. Add marinade and bring to the boil. Reduce heat and add spinach, tossing well. Cook until spinach has just collapsed.

To serve, squeeze spinach with tongs and place on each plate. Stack fish on top and drizzle with remaining marinade. Serve salsa separately or pile on top of fish.

Note   Orange roughy is also known as sea perch.

🐾 *kid friendly* on creamy potato mash without the spinach or salsa.

CRUSTED FISH FILLETS WITH ASPARAGUS ON CAULIFLOWER AND CELERIAC MASH

SERVES 2

prep time: 5 minutes

cook time: 8 minutes

½	cup almond meal
½	cup grated Parmesan
	sea salt
	cracked pepper
1	egg, lightly beaten
1	pound bream, carp or catfish fillets
	olive oil/olive oil spray
12	thick asparagus spears
	cauliflower and celeriac mash (see page 153, variation of *cauliflower mash*)
	lemon

Mix almond meal, Parmesan, salt and pepper on a plate. Dip fish in egg then roll in almond mixture. Heat a non-stick frying pan over medium to high heat. When hot, spray or brush well with oil and add fish. Cook for 3–4 minutes each side or until golden. Snap asparagus where it breaks naturally. Lightly steam for 2–3 minutes, then plunge immediately into cold water and drain.

To serve, place mash on each plate and lie asparagus with spear heads together across the mash. Place fish on an angle over asparagus and add 2 lemon wedges.

Note   Do not overcook asparagus as it loses texture, color and flavor. Fish fillets come in a range of sizes. If you have large fillets, cut them into 2 or 3 long pieces – you may need additional almond and Parmesan mixture.

Variations   Use broccoli and parsnip mash instead of cauliflower and celeriac mash (although it will cost you a few extra carbs), and green beans when asparagus is unavailable. Add 1 tablespoon finely chopped thyme to almond mixture, and use flaked almonds or crushed macadamia nut for a different texture and taste.

kid friendly with a simple potato mash and snow peas instead of asparagus. Before cooking fish, add a teaspoon of butter to the oil.

THAI FISH WITH COCONUT MILK AND SNOW PEAS

SERVES 4

prep time: 15 minutes

cook time: 10 minutes

2	handfuls bean sprouts
4	John Dory or snapper fillets (about 8 ounces each)
1	tablespoon peanut oil
2	stalks lemongrass (optional), finely chopped (white part only)
4	handfuls snow peas (9 ounces), tops trimmed
1	handful basil, finely chopped
4	handfuls baby spinach

Marinade

1	teaspoon green curry paste
1	tablespoon fish sauce
1	cup light coconut milk

Soak bean sprouts in fresh water for at least 10 minutes. Mix curry paste, fish sauce and coconut milk. Add fish and marinate for at least 15 minutes and up to an hour. Heat a non-stick wok or frying pan over medium heat. When hot, brush or spray with 2 teaspoons peanut oil and add fillets, retaining marinade. Cook for 2–3 minutes each side. Remove and keep warm. Wipe pan clean. Add remaining oil and increase heat. Add lemongrass and stirfry for 1 minute. Reduce heat and add marinade, snow peas, bean sprouts and basil. Return fish to wok. Cover and gently simmer for 1–2 minutes. Remove immediately from heat and serve.

To serve, place spinach on each plate, with fish on top. Spoon over vegetables and drizzle with marinade.

Note The intensity of the curry paste you use will depend on the brand. Follow the directions on the package or start with half a teaspoon and add gradually to obtain desired heat, if you're unsure. Once it is too hot there is little you can do to take the spice out!

Variations Use green or long beans with tops trimmed instead of snow peas. For extra kick, add a small red chile, seeded and finely sliced, or add 2 crushed lime leaves with the lemongrass. (See also variations on page 91.)

TARRAGON CHICKEN, LEEK AND BACON

SERVES 4

prep time: 10 minutes

cook time: 40 minutes

8	skinless chicken thighs with bone
3	bacon strips
2	tablespoons freshly chopped tarragon
	good pinch of sea salt
	cracked pepper
1	tablespoon olive oil
2	leeks, cut into ¾-inch slices
1	large carrot, cut into ¾-inch diagonals
2	stalks celery, cut into ¾-inch diagonals
1	cup chicken stock
1	teaspoon Dijon mustard
2	bay leaves
2	tablespoons low-fat sour cream or buttermilk (optional)
4	large handfuls baby spinach

Preheat oven to 350°F. Remove visible fat from chicken and bacon. Chop bacon into ¾-inch cubes. Mix tarragon with salt and pepper and sprinkle over chicken. Heat a large cast-iron casserole over medium to high heat and when hot, brush with or add oil. Add leek, carrot and celery and cook until leek is soft. Remove vegetables and add more oil to casserole. Add chicken and cook for 2 minutes each side. Add bacon and cook for a further 2 minutes. Return vegetables to casserole and add chicken stock, mustard and bay leaves. Cover and bake in oven for 30 minutes or simmer on stovetop for 45 minutes. Remove bay leaves.

To serve, place a handful of spinach in each bowl with chicken pieces on top. Ladle vegetables over spinach and dollop with sour cream.

Variations   Instead of spinach you can use arugula, creamed spinach (see chapter 6) and sautéed, shredded cabbage or sauerkraut. Add 2 zucchini cut into ¾-inch diagonals or 8 ounces button mushrooms, quartered, when cooking other vegetables.

🐛 *kid friendly* served on rice or noodles without the spinach.

CHICKEN WITH ROASTED PEPPERS AND OLIVES

SERVES 4

prep time: 30 minutes

cook time: 35 minutes

1	yellow pepper, halved, seeds and pith removed
1	green pepper, halved, seeds and pith removed
1	red pepper, halved, seeds and pith removed
1	tablespoon olive oil
1	yellow onion, cut into small wedges, retaining base
8	skinless chicken thigh fillets, cut into $1\frac{1}{2}$-inch squares
$\frac{1}{2}$	cup white wine
1	tablespoon tomato paste
14	ounces canned peeled, diced tomatoes (no added sugar)
1	tablespoon capers
12	kalamata olives
4	anchovy fillets, finely chopped
	cilantro, parsley and lemon salsa (optional) (see page 172)

Preheat grill to high or oven to 425°F. Place peppers on a tray lined with parchment paper cut-side down and bake or grill for 25 minutes or until blackened and blistered. Remove and place in a plastic bag for 10 minutes. Heat a large cast-iron casserole over medium heat. When hot, add oil and onion and cook until soft. Add chicken and cook for 3–4 minutes, tossing regularly. Add wine and allow liquid to reduce a little. Add tomato paste, tomatoes, capers, olives and anchovy fillets. Cover, reduce heat and simmer. Remove peppers from bag, peel and cut into 1-inch squares. Add to pot and simmer over heat or bake in moderate oven for 30 minutes or until chicken is cooked.

To serve, ladle chicken and vegetables into large bowls and sprinkle a few teaspoons of salsa over the top.

Note   To save time, simply slice peppers into long strips and cook with onion. It's still delicious but without the deeper flavor that comes from roasting.

Variations   Place a handful of arugula or spinach in each bowl before adding chicken and vegetables or serve on a sweet potato mash (see page 154, variation of pumpkin and ginger mash) for a higher-carb option.

🐾 *kid friendly* without capers or olives and served on rice or a simple mash.

ROAST CHICKEN, PEAR AND THYME ON CREAMED SPINACH

SERVES 4

prep time: 5 minutes

cook time: 60 minutes

4	skinless chicken leg-thigh sections (with bone)
	olive oil/olive oil spray
8	sprigs thyme
4	cloves garlic, sliced (skin on)
	sea salt
	cracked pepper
2	red onions, cut into wedges, retaining base
8	baby carrots, trimmed with ¾-inch green leaves intact
1	Bosc pear, sliced vertically into 8 long segments
¼	cup verjuice
	creamed spinach (see page 141)

Preheat oven to 400°F. Place chicken in a large cast-iron casserole or non-stick baking dish or dish lined with parchment paper. Spray or brush generously with oil and sprinkle with thyme, garlic, salt and pepper. Bake for 15 minutes and then add onion, carrot and pear. Spray or brush with a little more oil and toss well. Bake for a further 45 minutes or until chicken, vegetables and pear are golden and cooked through, tossing regularly. Five minutes prior to serving, remove from oven and add verjuice. Return to oven for 5 minutes.

To serve, spoon creamed spinach onto a large platter and arrange chicken and vegetables on top and serve at the table. Pour pan juices into a warm jug and serve at the table.

Note   Use white wine if verjuice is not available.

Variations   Replace pear with a ripe peach sliced into segments or use parsnip instead of carrot. This will create a very different flavor.

🌸 *kid friendly* served on a bed of mash.

CHICKEN SIMMERED WITH ORANGE, PUY LENTILS AND VEGETABLES

SERVES 4

prep time: 7 minutes

cook time: 50 minutes

8	**skinless chicken thigh fillets**
1	**tablespoon olive oil**
1	**onion, finely chopped**
4	**stalks celery, finely chopped**
1	**carrot, finely chopped**
2	**cups chicken stock**
½	**cup fresh orange juice**
¼	**cup Puy lentils or French green lentils**
1	**tablespoon fresh tarragon**
2	**tablespoons orange zest**
2	**cloves garlic, finely chopped**
4	**handfuls baby spinach**
	cracked pepper

Remove all visible fat from chicken and cut fillets in half vertically. Heat a large cast-iron casserole over medium to high heat. When hot, add oil, onion, celery and carrot. Reduce heat and cook for 5 minutes, stirring regularly. Add stock and orange juice and bring to the boil. Reduce to a low simmer and add chicken, lentils, tarragon, zest and garlic. Simmer, covered, for 45 minutes or until chicken and lentils are cooked.

To serve, place a handful of spinach in 4 bowls and ladle chicken and vegetables over the top.

Note   Puy lentils, or French green lentils, are higher in iron and magnesium than other lentils. They also have a thinner skin, so require less cooking, and hold their form better. These lentils have less starch and are therefore lower in carbohydrates. Their great taste and good fiber content make them worth the extra expense. Now not exclusively produced in Le Puy, France, French green lentils are more affordable and readily available at most supermarkets and delicatessens.

Variation   Dollop a tablespoon of light tzatziki or low-fat plain yogurt over chicken and vegetables.
Serve on a bed of warm sauerkraut or pumpkin and ginger mash (see page 154).

☘ *kid friendly* without lentils and served on a bed of brown rice or noodles.

BARBECUED CHICKEN WITH WATERMELON AND CUCUMBER SALSA

SERVES 4

prep time: 15 minutes

cook time: 10 minutes

8   **skinless chicken thigh fillets**
8   **large field or Chantarelle mushrooms, stalks removed**
     lime, garlic and soy marinade **(see page 174)**
     olive oil/olive oil spray
4   **handfuls arugula**
     watermelon and cucumber salsa **(see page 171)**

Remove any visible fat from chicken. Add chicken and mushrooms to marinade and let stand for at least 15 minutes. Heat barbecue to medium to high or place a griddle pan over medium to high heat. When hot, brush or spray with oil, remove chicken and mushrooms from marinade and place on barbecue. Barbecue chicken for 4–5 minutes each side or until cooked. Add mushrooms for 2–3 minutes each side.

To serve, place a handful of arugula on each plate, add 2 mushrooms and stack chicken on top. Spoon salsa over chicken.

Variation   Use mango and avocado salsa or avocado and tomato instead of watermelon and cucumber salsa. This is also delicious with roasted beet dip (see page 35) and barbecued vegetables (see page 152).

🐾 *kid friendly* with rice and salsa but without the cilantro.

CHICKEN, WATER CHESTNUT AND MUSHROOM LETTUCE WRAPS

SERVES 4

prep time: 30 minutes

cook time: 15 minutes

1	handful fresh bean sprouts
4	tablespoons slivered almonds or cashews
1	tablespoon sesame oil
1	tablespoon grated ginger
1	clove garlic, finely chopped
6	green onions, finely chopped
3	stalks celery, finely chopped
1	pound lean ground chicken (breast)
6	ounces shiitake mushrooms or 8 ounces button mushrooms, finely chopped
½	cup water chestnuts, finely chopped
2	handfuls mint, finely chopped
3	tablespoons mirin or dry sherry
2	tablespoons light soy sauce
	iceberg lettuce or baby romaine

Soak bean sprouts in water for at least 10 minutes. Preheat oven to 425°F. Roughly crush almonds and place on a tray lined with parchment paper. Bake for 10–15 minutes (only 7 minutes for cashews) or until golden. Heat a large non-stick wok or frying pan over medium to high heat. When hot, add oil, ginger, garlic and green onion and cook for 1 minute. Add celery and cook for a further minute. Add chicken and cook for 4–5 minutes. Add mushrooms and water chestnuts and cook for 2 more minutes. Add half the mint, mirin and soy sauce and stir. Add drained bean sprouts, reduce heat and simmer, covered, for 4–5 minutes. Cut lettuce in half and carefully peel off leaves.

To serve, place 2 lettuce "cups" on each plate and spoon in mixture. Sprinkle with almonds and remaining mint.

Note   Mirin is not strictly a low-carbohydrate condiment so don't use more than is suggested here. Dried mushrooms, soaked in water or stock, can be used instead of fresh in this recipe.

Variation   Use lean ground pork instead of chicken or try baby romaine instead of iceberg.

kid friendly using button mushrooms without the mint and served on a bed of rice or noodles.

MOROCCAN CHICKEN WITH PUMPKIN AND CILANTRO

SERVES 6

prep time: 10 minutes

cook time: 75–90 minutes

12	skinless chicken thigh fillets
2	cups pumpkin (10½ ounces) or sweet potato, cut into 1-inch chunks
1	large leek, cut into ¾-inch slices, or 2 red onions, cut into wedges, retaining base
1	red pepper, cut into 1-inch pieces
½	cup cooked Great Northern, cannellini or flageolet beans (optional)
3–4	cups chicken stock
1	cup snow peas or sugar snaps
1	handful freshly chopped parsley

2	handfuls cilantro
8	tablespoons low-fat ricotta or low-fat plain yogurt (optional)
4	handfuls arugula or spinach

Moroccan Paste

1	teaspoon ginger powder
1	teaspoon cumin
1	teaspoon paprika
1	teaspoon sambal oelek (chile paste)
1	teaspoon water

Preheat oven to 400°F. Mix spices and add water to make a paste. Remove any visible fat from chicken and arrange in a large casserole dish or baking tray (about 11 x 14-inch) in a single layer. Spread paste over chicken pieces. Place pumpkin, leek, pepper and beans around chicken and add stock to just cover ingredients. Bake for 1¼–1½ hours. After 40–45 minutes, turn vegetables that are browning. Cover with foil if contents start to burn. Roughly chop half the cilantro. Five minutes prior to removing from oven, add snow peas, parsley and chopped cilantro and gently mix.

To serve, place a handful of arugula on each plate with chicken on top and ladle vegetables over chicken. Dollop a tablespoon of ricotta on top and sprinkle over remaining coriander.

Note The pumpkin and beans are not strictly low-carbohydrate fare. If you are trying to shed pounds and reduce your carbs, replace beans with Puy lentils or soybeans and instead of pumpkin try zucchini, turnip or carrot. The quantity of stock used will depend on the size of the dish or tray but try to have the chicken and vegetables fitting snugly in a single layer. This dish is inspired by my friend Toni. See picture of this dish opposite.

THAI GREEN CHICKEN CURRY WITH SPINACH AND BEAN SPROUTS

SERVES 4

prep time: 15–20 minutes

cook time: 10 minutes

8	mini pappadams (optional)
1	cup pumpkin, chopped into ¾-inch cubes
1	pound skinless chicken thigh fillets
2	teaspoons peanut oil
½–1	teaspoon green curry paste
1	cup low-fat coconut milk
½	cup chicken stock
1	tablespoon fish sauce
2	handfuls basil, roughly chopped
2	handfuls fresh bean sprouts (about 8 ounces)
3	handfuls spinach (about 4 ounces)

Cook pappadams in microwave following instructions on the package or for 2 minutes on high. Lightly steam pumpkin until just soft on the outside. Remove any visible fat from chicken and cut into 1-inch chunks. Heat a wok or large non-stick frying pan over medium to high heat. When hot, add oil and curry paste. Combine well and heat for a few seconds. Increase heat, add chicken and cook for 2–3 minutes. Add pumpkin and cook for a further 2–3 minutes. Reduce heat, add coconut milk, stock and fish sauce. Simmer for a further 2 minutes or until chicken is cooked. Add basil, bean sprouts and spinach and stir gently for 1 minute.

Serve immediately in deep soup bowls with pappadams on top.

Note   The quantity of curry paste used will vary greatly depending on the brand. Be guided by the instructions. It's a good idea to tread cautiously and start with as little as half a teaspoon. Do not boil coconut milk as liquid will separate.

Variations   Add 2 finely sliced lemongrass stalks (first 2½–3 inches) to the oil and curry paste mixture. Add 2 handfuls green or long beans, topped and lightly steamed. Make this easy salsa to give the dish an extra dimension: finely chop ½ red onion, 2 tomatoes, 1 English cucumber and a handful of cilantro and dollop on top with a drizzle.

Opposite: Turkey Breast in Almond and Parmesan with Fresh Asparagus (page 93)

TANDOORI CHICKEN WITH CUCUMBER SALAD

SERVES 4

prep time: 15 minutes

cook time: 35 minutes

4	skinless chicken breast fillets (about 8 ounces each)
8	mini pappadams
2	roma tomatoes
1	mango, sliced into long, thin wedges
1	avocado, sliced into long, thin wedges
	cucumber with yogurt and lime (see page 130)

Marinade

2	tablespoons tandoori paste
2	tablespoons low-fat plain yogurt

Preheat oven to 400°F. To make marinade, mix tandoori paste and yogurt together. Remove any visible fat from chicken and cut breast with several deep slits. Cover well with marinade. Refrigerate for at least 15 minutes or marinate overnight if possible. Place chicken in a baking dish lined with parchment paper or on a non-stick baking tray and bake for 35 minutes or until cooked. Cook pappadams in microwave following instructions on the pack.

To serve, layer tomato, mango and avocado on each plate and arrange chicken on top. Spoon over cucumber salad and place pappadams to the side.

Note   See picture of this dish opposite page 155.

Variations   Remember that mangoes are quite high in carbohydrates, so replace with a little sliced red onion and cucumber if you are being very careful about your carbohydrate intake. Barbecue chicken for a different flavor. Serve with light tzatziki instead of cucumber salad for a convenient alternative.

TURKEY BREAST IN ALMOND AND PARMESAN WITH FRESH ASPARAGUS

SERVES 2

prep time: 5 minutes

cook time: 10 minutes

4	tablespoons grated Parmesan
2	tablespoons almond meal
	cracked pepper
2	turkey breast fillet slices or cutlets (about 6 ounces each)
1	egg, lightly beaten
	olive oil/olive oil spray
2	teaspoons butter
12	thick asparagus spears
2	vine-ripened tomatoes, cut into ¾-inch slices
2	teaspoons balsamic vinegar
2	tablespoons basil, torn
	extra virgin olive oil
	sea salt

Combine Parmesan with almond meal and cracked pepper. Spread mixture onto a board. Dip turkey into egg and press firmly into almond mixture. Refrigerate for up to 1 hour if you have time. Heat a large non-stick frying pan over medium heat. When hot, brush or spray well with a little oil and add butter. Add fillets and cook for 2–3 minutes each side or until golden and cooked. Meanwhile snap ends off asparagus and lightly steam or microwave for 2–3 minutes or until just cooked and crisp. Plunge briefly into cold water to retain color, then slice asparagus lengthwise. Add tomato to pan. Drizzle with 1 teaspoon balsamic vinegar and scatter basil over the top. Cook for 1–2 minutes each side.

To serve, place asparagus on each plate. Slice fillet into thick diagonals, place on top of asparagus and arrange tomato slices to the side. Drizzle with remaining balsamic and a little extra virgin olive oil and season to taste.

Note   Pre-packaged, grated Parmesan is never as tasty as the real thing, but it's a good alternative if you're pushed for time. The cutlets recommended here and in the following recipes are about ½–¾-inches thick and don't require a lot of cooking. See picture of this dish opposite page 91.

Variations   When asparagus is unavailable, serve with some freshly steamed beans. Use roasted red pepper instead of tomatoes or some avocado mash (see page 173).

🐛 *kid friendly* served on a bed of mash or with chips.

TURKEY CHOPS WITH ROASTED RED PEPPER SAUCE

prep time: 5 minutes

cook time: 20 minutes

2	**turkey thigh chops**
	herb salt (optional) or sea salt
2	**large field mushrooms, stalks removed**
	olive oil/olive oil spray
8	**ounces broccolini**
4	**tablespoons *roasted red pepper sauce* (see page 161)**

Preheat oven to 425°F. Remove visible fat from chops and sprinkle lightly with herb salt. Spray mushrooms with oil and place flesh side up on tray. Bake for 20 minutes. Heat a non-stick griddle or frying pan over medium heat. When hot, brush or spray with oil and add turkey. Cook for 2–3 minutes each side or until cooked. Lightly steam or microwave broccolini.

Place mushroom on plate with turkey on top. Arrange broccolini on the side. Dollop sauce over turkey and serve.

Variation   Replace mushrooms with sautéed mushrooms and garlic (see page 140).

🌼 *kid friendly* without the mushrooms or roasted red pepper sauce and served with a mash and tomato sauce.

TURKEY, EGGPLANT, TOMATO AND BASIL STACK

SERVES 4

prep time: 10 minutes

cook time: 30 minutes

4	slices eggplant, cut horizontally, $\frac{1}{3}$-inch thick
	olive oil/olive oil spray
	sea salt
4	turkey breast fillet slices or cutlets (about 6 ounces each)
2	tablespoons *roasted tomato sauce* (see page 160)
2	tomatoes, cut into $\frac{1}{3}$-inch slices
4	tablespoons basil, finely chopped
4	tablespoons grated mozzarella

Preheat oven to 425°F. Place eggplant on a tray lined with parchment paper. Spray or brush with oil and sprinkle with salt. Bake for 20–25 minutes or until golden. Heat a non-stick frying pan over medium to high heat. When hot, brush or spray with oil and add turkey. Cook for 1 minute each side, then remove from heat. Remove eggplant from oven and spread with a thin layer of tomato sauce. Arrange turkey and then tomato on top of tomato sauce. Sprinkle over basil and then mozzarella. Bake until turkey is cooked through, about 5–10 minutes.

To serve, arrange on plate and serve with a simple green salad.

Note   For a short cut, use cooked slices of turkey breast fillet available from most supermarkets and delicatessens. It will only need about 5 minutes in the oven.

Variation   Replace turkey with veal scaloppini of a similar size.

TURKEY WITH PROSCIUTTO, SAGE AND BOCCONCINI

SERVES 2

prep time: 5 minutes

cook time: 35–40 minutes

2   **turkey breast fillet slices or cutlets (about 6 ounces each)**

4   **sage leaves**

2   **vine-ripened tomatoes, cut into $\frac{1}{3}$-inch slices**

2   **large bocconcini balls, cut into $\frac{1}{3}$-inch slices**

4   **slices prosciutto**

1   **leek, cut into $\frac{1}{3}$-inch slices**

$\frac{1}{2}$ **cup vegetable stock**

    olive oil

    sea salt

    cracked pepper

Preheat oven to 400°F. On half of each fillet stack 2 sage leaves, 1 slice tomato and 2 slices bocconcini. Fold other half over sage, tomato and cheese. Wrap 1 slice prosciutto around turkey to secure filling and tuck ends under. Wrap a second slice across fillet to form a cross and again tuck the ends under. Place leek and remaining tomato in a small non-stick rectangular cake pan. Place turkey parcels on top of leek and tomato and add stock. Bake for 35–40 minutes or until cooked.

    To serve, place leek on each plate with tomato on top. Arrange turkey on vegetables and serve.

Variation   Use veal scaloppini instead of turkey breast and feta or a little goat cheese marinated in oil instead of bocconcini balls.

TURKEY WITH BRAISED FENNEL

SERVES 2

prep time: 5 minutes

cook time: 10 minutes

4	baby fennel or ½ medium fennel with a handful of leaves, stalks discarded
	pinch of sea salt
2	turkey breast fillet slices or cutlets (about 6 ounces each)
	olive oil/olive oil spray
1	cup vegetable stock
1	carrot, shredded
1	tablespoon low-fat sour cream
2	handfuls spinach

Finely chop fennel leaves and finely slice fennel bulbs. Mix 2 tablespoons leaves with salt on a cutting board and firmly press turkey fillets into mixture until well covered. Heat a non-stick frying pan over medium heat. When hot, brush or spray well with oil and add turkey. Cook for 1 minute each side or until just cooked. Remove and keep warm. In same pan, increase heat, spray or brush well with oil and add fennel bulb. Cook for 3–4 minutes or until golden. Add stock and carrot. Bring to the boil, then reduce heat and cook for 3 minutes. Remove from heat and add sour cream, mixing well.

To serve, place a handful of fresh spinach on each plate, spoon over fennel and carrot mixture and place turkey on top. Drizzle sauce over turkey and vegetables.

Variation Replace turkey with chicken, veal or pork fillets and adjust cooking time.

TURKEY, ORANGE AND MINT WITH WILTED SPINACH

SERVES 2

prep time: 5 minutes

cook time: 10 minutes

2	turkey breast fillet slices or cutlets (about 6 ounces each)
	sea salt
	cracked pepper
	olive oil/olive oil spray
1	tablespoon orange zest
¼	cup fresh orange juice
1	clove garlic, finely chopped
2	tablespoons mint, finely chopped
¼	cup chicken stock
1	teaspoon freshly grated ginger
8	handfuls spinach
8	baby carrots, with ¾-inch greens intact

Lightly season turkey with salt and pepper. Heat a non-stick frying pan over medium to high heat. When hot, brush or spray with oil and add turkey. Cook for 2 minutes each side or until golden and just cooked. Remove and keep warm. Lightly steam or microwave baby carrots. Combine orange zest, juice, garlic, mint and chicken stock and whisk. Heat a large saucepan over medium heat. Add 2 teaspoons water and spinach and cook, covered, for 2 minutes or until spinach has wilted, stirring regularly to stop spinach sticking. Add orange mixture to original frying pan and bring to the boil. Reduce heat and return turkey to frying pan for 1–2 minutes.

To serve, place spinach on each plate and arrange turkey on top. Drizzle with orange sauce and scatter baby carrots around.

Variation Serve on pumpkin and ginger mash or sweet potato mash (see page 154) for a slightly higher-carbohydrate meal, and serve spinach in a separate bowl.

BEEF TENDERLOIN ON FENNEL WITH AVOCADO MASH

SERVES 4

prep time: 20 minutes

cook time: 25 minutes

1   **pound beef tenderloin or 4 steaks**
     sea salt
     cracked pepper
1   **red pepper, cut in half, seeds and pith removed**
1   **ripe avocado**
     olive oil/olive oil spray
     fennel in Parmesan and almond (see page 144)

Preheat oven to 425°F or to high. Slice beef tenderloin into 4 thick, even slices and season with salt and pepper. Place pepper cut-side down on a tray lined with parchment paper and bake or grill for 20–25 minutes or until blackened and blistered. Place in plastic bag for 10 minutes. Remove skin and slice into long, thin strips. Mash avocado and season with a little salt and pepper. Heat a non-stick griddle pan over medium to high heat. When hot, brush or spray with oil and add beef. Cook for 2–3 minutes each side or until medium rare, or longer according to taste.

To serve, place a fennel slice on each plate and put beef on top. Dollop 2 tablespoons avocado over beef and scatter pepper strips over the dish.

Note   Cooking time will vary depending on the thickness of meat.

Variations   Use tomato and avocado salsa instead of avocado and red pepper strips or try avocado mash (see page 173). Instead of fennel in Parmesan and almond, simply slice fennel finely, sauté in a little olive oil and top with shaved Parmesan and cracked pepper. Alternatively, use large field mushrooms roasted in the oven or chargrilled with garlic and oil or pesto as a base for the meat and mash. Substitute sliced lamb fillets for beef and adjust the cooking time.

kid friendly served on a broccoli and parsnip mash.

SHAVED BEEF ON BROCCOLI AND PARSNIP MASH

SERVES 6

prep time: 10 minutes

cook time: 15 minutes

1½	pounds sirloin or tenderloin steak		3	tablespoons *roasted tomato sauce* (see page 160) or tomato paste
	sea salt		2	teaspoons peanut butter
	cracked pepper		2	tablespoons Dijon mustard
2	tablespoons olive oil		3	tablespoons dill pickle, finely sliced
2	cloves garlic, minced		½	cup light evaporated milk
1	onion, sliced			*broccoli and parsnip mash*
10	ounces mushrooms, sliced			(see page 155)
½	cup red wine		12	ounces green beans
1	cup beef stock			

Finely slice steak and then cut each slice into $^3/_4$-inch widths. Lightly season with salt and pepper. Heat a large cast-iron casserole over high heat. Add 1 tablespoon oil and when hot, add beef in small batches, placing each piece separately in pan. Sear for a few seconds on each side, then remove to paper towels. Add additional oil (if required) and repeat until all beef is cooked. Reduce heat and add garlic and onion. Cook for 2 minutes or until onion has softened. Add mushrooms and cook for 3 more minutes. Increase heat and add wine. Bring to the boil and reduce liquid slightly. Add stock, tomato sauce, peanut butter and mustard and stir until combined. Return meat and pickles to pan and stir. Simmer for 2 minutes or until meat is warm. Add milk and stir. Do not boil, as liquid will curdle and separate.

To serve, dollop mash into large shallow soup bowls and spoon beef and mushrooms over mash. Serve with green beans.

Variation   Serve with a simple green salad instead of mash. This will reduce the total carbohydrates of the dish.

☠ *kid friendly* without mushrooms or dill pickle, and served on noodles or mash.

CORIANDER-CRUSTED BEEF TENDERLOIN WITH BABY BEETS, GREEN BEANS AND GOAT CHEESE

SERVES 4

prep time: 10 minutes

cook time: 20 minutes

3	tablespoons coriander seeds
1	teaspoon sea salt
1	teaspoon cracked pepper
1	pound beef tenderloin
	olive oil/olive oil spray
	baby beets and green beans with goat cheese (see page 156)

Preheat oven to 375°F. Finely crush coriander seeds, salt and pepper with mortar and pestle and spread mixture on a board. Roll beef firmly across seasoning. Heat a cast-iron frying or griddle pan over high heat. When hot, spray with oil and add beef. Cook for 3 minutes each side or until beef forms golden crust. Take off heat and place on a tray lined with parchment paper. Bake for 15 minutes or until medium rare, or longer according to taste. Remove beef and let rest for 10–15 minutes. Cut beef into $3/4$-inch slices.

To serve, place beef on each plate and pile beets, green beans and goat cheese on the side or serve sliced beef on a large platter with vegetables scattered around. Drizzle natural juices over beef.

Note   See picture of this dish opposite page 123.

Variations   Use lamb fillets instead of beef and reduce baking time, as lamb fillets are generally smaller. Serve with green beans and sweet potato and ginger mash (see page 154, variation of pumpkin and ginger mash) as a bed for the meat. For a lower-carb and lower-fat alternative, use cauliflower mash (see page 153) and serve with a simple green salad.

🌷 *kid friendly* without coriander seeds. Forget the side vegetables, but cut green beans in half and stick in mash like a pincushion.

T-BONE STEAK WITH HORSERADISH CREAM ON SHREDDED ZUCCHINI

SERVES 2

prep time: 15 minutes

cook time: 10 minutes

1 **thick T-bone steak (1 inch) (about 1 pound)**
olive oil/olive oil spray
sea salt
2 **zucchini**
cracked pepper
horseradish cream **(see page 167)**
herb-salted turnip chips **(see page 151)**

Remove all visible fat from steak. Lightly brush steak with oil and sprinkle with a little salt. Slice zucchini lengthwise into long, thin strips with a wide vegetable peeler. Preheat a non-stick griddle pan or cast-iron frying pan over high heat and when hot, lightly brush or spray with olive oil and add steak. Cook for 2 minutes each side for medium rare, or longer according to taste. Remove from heat and let stand. Reduce heat and lightly brush or spray griddle with oil. Add zucchini and cook for 2 minutes each side or until soft and golden.

To serve, divide steak and place on plates. Arrange zucchini strips on top and stack turnip chips on the side. Dollop a few teaspoons of horseradish cream on the side.

Note   Barbecue steak for a different flavor, sealing meat and cooking zucchini first on the hot plate and then finishing meat on the grill. Chips will take 25–30 minutes so time your preparation and cooking of meat accordingly.

Variations   Replace turnip chips with celeriac or, for a higher-carbohydrate side dish, parsnip chips. Use Dijon mustard instead of horseradish cream. Steamed, baked or grilled whitefish also works well with this combination of zucchini, turnip chips and horseradish cream.

BEEF AND MUSHROOMS IN RED WINE

SERVES 4

prep time: 10 minutes

cook time: 60–90 minutes

1½	pounds stew, chuck or blade steak		1	pound peeled, diced tomatoes
	sea salt		2	cloves garlic, crushed
	cracked pepper		2	bay leaves
2	red onions		6	anchovies, chopped
2	sprigs rosemary or thyme		1	tablespoon horseradish sauce
1	tablespoon olive oil		½	cup red wine
2	carrots, sliced into ¾-inch diagonals		1	cup beef stock
8	ounces field, flat or portobello mushrooms, stalks removed and halved			

Preheat oven to 350°F. Remove all visible fat from beef and cut into 1½-inch cubes. Season with salt and pepper. Peel onions, retaining base, and cut vertically into 8 wedges. Tear rosemary into ¾-inch sprigs. Heat a large cast-iron casserole over medium to high heat. When hot, add oil, onion and carrot. Cook for 2–3 minutes, stirring regularly until softened. Add remaining ingredients to casserole, stir well and bake for 1–1½ hours with lid on.

To serve, ladle beef and vegetables into large soup bowls.

Note   This dish is inspired by my mother's many delicious casseroles. Don't be put off by the long cooking time; this dish can be made during the day and is even better the following day. Avoid pre-cut meat from the supermarket as the pieces are generally too small and will result in a chewy texture. See picture of this dish opposite page 171.

Variations   Serve on creamed spinach, broccoli and parsnip mash (see chapter 6) or sauerkraut or with a simple green salad. For a more impressive version, use 12 shallots (instead of onions), peeled but with their bases intact. This is a little more time-consuming so don't consider it if you are pressed for time.

BEEF AND BACON BURGERS WITH BEETS AND ROASTED TOMATO SAUCE

SERVES 4

prep time: 10 minutes

cook time: 45 minutes

2	beets	1	egg	
	good pinch of sea salt	2	ounces almond meal	
1	pound lean ground beef		cracked pepper	
2	bacon strips, trimmed and finely chopped		olive oil/olive oil spray	
½	red onion, finely chopped	1	vine-ripened tomato, sliced into ⅓-inch widths	
4	halves sun-dried or semi-dried tomatoes, finely chopped	8	iceberg lettuce leaves	
2	tablespoons tomato paste	8	tablespoons *roasted tomato sauce* (see page 160) or Dijon mustard or *horseradish cream* (see page 167)	
1	tablespoon Dijon mustard (optional)			
1	small red chile (optional), seeded and finely chopped			

Preheat oven to 425°F. Cut beets in half horizontally and place each half on a separate piece of foil, then salt. Wrap tightly and bake for 40–45 minutes or until cooked through. Meanwhile, combine beef, bacon, onion, sun-dried tomato, tomato paste, mustard, chile, egg, almond meal, salt and pepper in a large bowl. Mix well, then roll into palm-size burgers (to make about 12–14). Let stand covered and refrigerated for up to 1 hour, if possible. Heat a non-stick frying pan over medium to high heat. When hot, brush or spray with oil and add burgers. Cook for 2–3 minutes each side or until lightly browned and cooked through. Keep warm in oven at low heat. Cut cooked beets horizontally into ⅓-inch widths.

To serve, place 2 lettuce cups on each plate with beet and tomato slices inside. Place a burger on top and a dollop of tomato sauce on top of burger.

Note   Peeling beets is time-consuming and unnecessary; removing the skin deprives you of extra fiber.

Variation   This recipe works just as well with lean ground chicken, pork or veal instead of beef.

☠ *kid friendly* without mustard and chile. For another great family dish, place 2 cups roasted tomato sauce, 1 can tomatoes and ½-cup chicken stock in a cast-iron casserole. Mix well and bring to the boil. Reduce heat to a simmer and gently place golf-ball-sized burgers in sauce. Cover and cook for 15–20 minutes. Meanwhile, finely chop 2 cloves garlic and a large handful of flat-leaf parsley. Add to casserole 5 minutes prior to serving. Season to taste and sprinkle with Parmesan.

BEEF BOLOGNESE AND RICOTTA ON EGGPLANT SLICES

SERVES 4

prep time: 5 minutes

cook time: 40 minutes

1	tablespoon olive oil	2	cups chicken stock
1	onion, finely chopped	1	tablespoon Worcestershire sauce
2	stalks celery, finely chopped	2	cloves garlic, crushed
2	carrots, finely chopped	2	eggplants
1	pound lean ground beef		olive oil/olive oil spray
2	tablespoons tomato paste		sea salt
1	pound canned peeled, diced tomatoes (no added sugar)	4	tablespoons low-fat ricotta cracked pepper
2	bay leaves		

Preheat oven to 450°F. Heat a large non-stick frying pan over medium heat and when hot, add oil, onion, celery and carrot. Cook for 4–5 minutes, stirring regularly. Move vegetables to one side of pan and add beef. Cook for 5 minutes or until browned. Add tomato paste, tomatoes, bay leaves, stock, Worcestershire sauce and garlic and bring to the boil. Reduce heat and simmer for at least half an hour and up to 2 hours. You will need to add extra stock for further cooking. Meanwhile slice eggplant lengthwise into $3/4$-inch slices. Place on a non-stick tray or tray lined with baking paper. Spray with olive oil and sprinkle with salt. Bake for 30 minutes or until golden.

To serve, place 2 eggplant slices on each plate and spoon the Bolognese sauce on top. Dollop a tablespoon of creamy ricotta over the Bolognese sauce and season with salt and pepper.

Note   Keep additional eggplant slices for lunch or a snack the next day. Beef is an excellent source of both iron and zinc. Dietary iron, found in meat, is readily absorbed. Zinc is a trace mineral that fights infection and helps to prevent dandruff and dry skin.

Variations   Use ground veal, pork or chicken instead of beef but with these meats use light soy sauce instead of Worcestershire sauce. Replace ricotta with grated Parmesan or low-fat mozzarella. Sprinkle it over the Bolognese sauce and place in oven for a few minutes. Finely slice $1/2$ savoy cabbage instead of eggplant and sauté in a little olive oil over medium to high heat for a few minutes, then top with the Bolognese sauce.

kid friendly on pasta with Parmesan or mozzarella.

BEEF, LEMONGRASS AND BROCCOLINI STIRFRY

SERVES 4

prep time: 10 minutes

cook time: 15 minutes

2	tablespoons cashews or slivered almonds
1	red pepper
1–2	tablespoons peanut oil
1	pound beef tenderloin or sirloin, finely sliced
3	cloves garlic, finely chopped
3	stems lemongrass, finely sliced (first 2½-3 inches only)
1	small red chile, seeded and finely sliced
8	green onions, finely sliced
3	cups chopped broccolini (about 7 ounces)
3	tablespoons fish sauce
1	tablespoon light soy
1	large handful mint, freshly chopped
1	small handful Vietnamese mint (or peppermint), freshly torn

Preheat oven to 400°F. Place cashews on a non-stick baking tray or tray lined with parchment paper and bake for 10 minutes or until golden. Remove when cooked and lightly crush. Slice pepper into ³⁄₄-inch strips and then diagonally into ³⁄₄-inch pieces. Heat a non-stick wok or a large non-stick frying pan over medium to high heat. When hot, add or brush with a little oil. Add beef in small batches, placing each piece separately in pan. Sear each side quickly and remove onto paper towels. Repeat until all meat is cooked. Add a little more oil to pan and when hot, add garlic, lemongrass and chile. Cook for 1 minute, then add green onion, red pepper and broccolini. Cook for 1–2 minutes and then add fish sauce and soy. Reduce heat and simmer for 1–2 minutes, then return beef to pan. Add mint and toss gently.

To serve, spoon stirfry into large soup bowls and sprinkle with Vietnamese mint and cashews.

Note   When cooking meat you will need to add a little more oil with each batch.

Variations   Substitute 1 tablespoon grated ginger for lemongrass. Use broccoli if broccolini is unavailable or 20 thin asparagus spears (about 10½ ounces) cut diagonally into 2-inch pieces. Add 2 handfuls bean sprouts that have been soaked in cold water.

Opposite: Tarragon Pork with Verjuice and Peach (page 125)

MODERN VEAL TONNATO WITH SNOW PEAS

SERVES 4

prep time: 5 minutes

cook time: 5 minutes

4   veal loin steaks (about 6 ounces each) or 4 veal scaloppini (about 6 ounces each)
    sea salt
    cracked pepper
6   ounces canned tuna in oil, drained
2   tablespoons whole egg mayonnaise
2   teaspoons lemon juice
1   tablespoon capers
4   handfuls snow peas or sugar snap peas, topped
    olive oil/olive oil spray
10 handfuls spinach

Season veal with salt and pepper. Combine tuna with mayonnaise, lemon juice and capers to make a smooth paste. Lightly steam or microwave snow peas for 2–3 minutes or until just cooked and still crisp. Remove and plunge into cold water. Heat a griddle or non-stick frying pan over medium to high heat. When hot, brush or spray with oil and add veal. Cook for 2–3 minutes on each side or until cooked to your liking. Place spinach with a tablespoon of water in a large saucepan over medium heat. Cover and cook for 2–3 minutes or until just wilted.

To serve, squeeze excess liquid from spinach and place on each plate with veal on top. Place snow peas alongside and dollop tuna mixture on top of veal.

Variation   Use asparagus when in season or green beans, topped and lightly steamed.

🌼 *kid friendly* with mash or parsnip chips.

Opposite: Baked Salmon in Balsamic and Maple Syrup with Shaved Fennel (page 78)

CRUSTED VEAL SCALOPPINI WITH BROCCOLI AND PARSNIP MASH

SERVES 4

prep time: 25 minutes

cook time: 20 minutes

2	teaspoons *basil pesto* (optional) (see page 162)
4	veal scaloppini (about 6 ounces each)
4	tablespoons almond meal
4	tablespoons finely grated Parmesan
	sea salt
	cracked pepper
1	egg, lightly beaten
	olive oil/olive oil spray
2	teaspoons butter
1	pound green beans, topped
	broccoli and parsnip mash (see page 155)
	lemon

Finely spread pesto over the top of veal. Mix almond meal, Parmesan, salt and pepper. Dip veal in egg and then roll in almond meal and Parmesan. Heat a non-stick frying pan over medium to high heat. When hot, lightly spray or brush with oil and add butter. Add veal and cook for 1–2 minutes each side or longer according to taste. Lightly steam beans.

To serve, place mash on each plate with veal on top. Stack beans next to veal and serve with lemon wedges.

Note   For a better result, refrigerate crusted veal for at least half an hour prior to cooking.

Variations   Use balsamic tomatoes (see page 139) instead of mash for a lower-carbohydrate alternative or 8 handfuls wilted spinach or greens. For something quite different, spread a tablespoon of roasted tomato sauce (see page 160) on top of each piece of seared veal. Sprinkle with finely chopped basil and a tablespoon of grated low-fat mozzarella. Place under a grill for 2 minutes or until cheese melts.

kid friendly – probably better received without pesto.

VEAL WITH OLIVES AND LEMON ON EGGPLANT SLICES

SERVES 4

prep time: 10 minutes

cook time: 20–25 minutes

1	large or 2 small eggplant, cut vertically into ⅓-inch slices
	olive oil/olive oil spray
	sea salt
	cracked pepper
4	veal loin steaks
1	tablespoon capers
12	olives, pitted and halved lengthwise
2	tablespoons lemon juice
1	tablespoon lemon zest
2	tablespoons flat-leaf parsley, finely chopped
2	cloves garlic, crushed
2	vine-ripened tomatoes, sliced into ⅓-inch widths
4	handfuls arugula or spinach

Preheat oven to 425°F. Place eggplant on a non-stick tray or tray lined with parchment paper. Brush or spray with olive oil and sprinkle with a little salt. Bake for 20–25 minutes or until golden. Lightly salt and pepper veal. Heat a non-stick frying pan over medium to high heat. Brush or spray with olive oil and when pan is hot, add veal. Cook for 2–3 minutes on each side, or longer according to taste. Remove and keep warm. Add a teaspoon of olive oil to same pan. Add capers and olives and cook for 1 minute over medium heat. Remove from heat and add lemon juice, parsley and garlic to pan. Stir well.

To serve, stack eggplant slices in the middle of each plate with tomato slices, pile with arugula and arrange veal on top. Drizzle sauce, capers and olives over veal and sprinkle with lemon zest. Serve with simple green vegetables.

Variation   Use veal scaloppini instead of steaks or serve on broccoli and parsnip mash (see page 155) instead of eggplant. This will mean a few extra carbs, but it's a delicious change.

VEAL CHOPS WITH CAPERS, BASIL AND MINT SALSA

SERVES 4

prep time: 15 minutes

cook time: 10 minutes

4	veal chops or T-bone steaks (about 8 ounces each)
	sea salt
	cracked pepper
	olive oil/olive oil spray
8	tablespoons *capers, basil and mint salsa* (see page 172)
	broccoli, olives and feta (see page 157)

Remove all visible fat from chops or steaks. Season veal with salt and pepper. Heat a griddle or non-stick frying pan over medium to high heat. When hot, lightly spray or brush with oil and add veal. Cook for 4–5 minutes on each side or until medium rare.

To serve, place veal on each plate and dollop 2 tablespoons salsa on top. Scatter broccoli, olives and feta around veal and serve with a simple green salad.

Note   Try to have the meat as close to room temperature as possible before cooking.

Variations   Serve with broccoli and parsnip mash (see page 155) for a slightly higher-carbohydrate side dish or serve simply with $^1/_2$ shredded savoy cabbage sautéed in a little butter and 2 teaspoons mustard seed. Add 2 tomatoes, halved and grilled. Also delicious with sweet potato, parsnip or turnip chips (see page 151).

VEAL STACK WITH PROSCIUTTO, SPINACH AND TOMATO

SERVES 4

prep time: 5 minutes

cook time: 10 minutes

4	veal scaloppini (about 6 ounces each)
	sea salt
	cracked pepper
	olive oil/olive oil spray
8	large handfuls baby spinach
3	ripe tomatoes, cut into ⅓-inch slices
2	long slices prosciutto, cut lengthwise into equal halves
4	bocconcini balls, cut into ⅓-inch slices
4	handfuls green beans (about 8 ounces), topped
4	large basil leaves

Preheat oven grill to high. Season veal with salt and pepper. Heat a griddle or non-stick frying pan over medium to high heat. When hot, lightly spray or brush with oil and add veal. Cook for 1 minute each side or until just cooked. Remove and place on a non-stick tray or tray lined with parchment paper. Cover veal with a layer of spinach leaves, tomato slices, prosciutto and bocconcini. If prosciutto pieces are too long, trim ends and stack on top. Place under grill for 2–3 minutes or until cheese melts and is golden. Lightly steam beans. Place remaining spinach in a large saucepan with 1 tablespoon water over medium heat. Cover and cook for 2–3 minutes or until just wilted.

To serve, remove excess liquid from spinach and place in the center of each plate. Arrange veal on top, garnish with a basil leaf and serve green beans in a bowl.

Note   If veal pieces are large, cut each scaloppini in half. Each piece should be the size of your palm.

Variations   With a few simple ingredients, you can make this dish taste quite different. Use asparagus or snow peas instead of green beans. Substitute turkey or pork for veal. Place veal on a baked eggplant slice (see page 109) or scatter 12 sliced kalamata or green olives over tomato before topping with cheese. Spread veal with roasted tomato sauce (see page 160) instead of using tomato slices.

CHILE AND SOY CHARGRILLED VEAL WITH ZUCCHINI AND SWEET POTATO

SERVES 4

prep time: 5 minutes

cook time: 30 minutes

4	veal loin chops or veal T-bone steak (about 8 ounces each)
12	slices sweet potato ($\frac{1}{3}$-inch wide)
	olive oil/olive oil spray
4	zucchini, sliced lengthwise into long, thin strips

Chile and Soy Marinade

1	tablespoon sesame oil
2	tablespoons red wine vinegar
4	tablespoons light soy sauce
1	teaspoon chile paste with fermented soybean
2	tablespoons water
1	tablespoon tomato paste

Preheat oven to 425°F. Combine marinade ingredients and marinate chops for at least 1 hour or overnight if possible. Place sweet potato on a non-stick tray or tray lined with parchment paper and lightly spray or brush with olive oil. Bake for 25–30 minutes or until golden. Heat a non-stick griddle or frying pan over medium to high heat. When hot, lightly spray or brush with oil and add chops, retaining marinade. Cook for 3–4 minutes each side or until medium rare. Remove from heat and keep warm. Wipe pan and place over medium to high heat. Lightly spray or brush with oil and add zucchini. Cook for 4 minutes or until golden, shaking regularly. Meanwhile heat remaining marinade.

To serve, place zucchini in the center of each plate, with veal on top and 3 disks of sweet potato on each chop. Spoon over a little marinade.

Variations Use dry sherry as an alternative to red wine vinegar. Replace sweet potato with herb-salted turnip or celeriac chips (see page 151) for a lower-carbohydrate side dish.

VEAL RACK WITH FENNEL AND BROAD BEANS

SERVES 4

prep time: 10 minutes

cook time: 50 minutes

½ cup fresh broad beans (optional)
1 frenched veal rack (about 1½ pounds), with 4 cutlets
  sea salt
  cracked pepper
1 tablespoon olive oil
1 large or 2 small fennel
½ cup white wine or verjuice
3 bay leaves
4 sprigs rosemary
2 tablespoons buttermilk (optional) or light sour cream
  pumpkin and ginger mash (see page 154)

Preheat oven to 400°F. Place broad beans into boiling water and cook for 5 minutes or until tender. Remove and immerse in cold water. Slide beans out of skins (optional). Season veal with salt and pepper. Heat a large cast-iron casserole over medium to high heat. When hot, add oil and veal rack and cook for 3 minutes each side or until golden. Meanwhile, remove outer leaves of fennel, slice bulb in half lengthwise and cut each half into 4 wedges. Add fennel, white wine, bay leaves and rosemary to casserole. Cover and bake for 40 minutes until veal is medium rare, or longer according to taste. Add cooked beans 15 minutes before taking veal out of oven. Remove veal from casserole and allow meat to rest for 10–15 minutes. Return casserole to low heat and simmer. Just prior to serving add buttermilk. Cut meat into 4 cutlets.

To serve, dollop mash in the middle of each plate with veal on top. Spoon vegetables and sauce over meat. If there are only 2 or 3 cutlets, cut meat from bones and slice veal into 4 thick pieces. Place bones on the plates of those you know will enjoy them.

Note   If fresh broad beans are unavailable, use frozen broad beans. If fennel is unavailable, use 2 leeks sliced into ³/₄-inch widths. See picture of this dish opposite page 139.

Variations   Use ¹/₂-cup cooked or canned soy or cannellini beans (these beans do not need to have their skins removed) or French green lentils. Use fresh tarragon or thyme instead of rosemary and serve with any of the mashes. When you add fennel to casserole, add ¹/₂-cup dried mushrooms that have been softened in water.

VEAL SHANKS WITH CAULIFLOWER MASH AND HORSERADISH CREAM

SERVES 4

prep time: 30 minutes

cook time: 135 minutes

12	small veal shanks
	sea salt
	cracked pepper
	olive oil/olive oil spray
2	cloves garlic, crushed
8	ounces button mushrooms, quartered, or field mushrooms, chopped
4	stalks celery, finely chopped
1	large carrot, finely chopped
1	yellow onion, finely chopped
½	cup white wine
1	pound canned peeled, diced tomatoes or 2 cups *roasted tomato sauce* (see page 160)
3	cups chicken stock
2	sprigs rosemary
	cilantro, parsley and lemon salsa (optional) (see page 172)
	cauliflower mash with horseradish cream (see page 153)

Season shanks with salt and pepper. Preheat oven to 350°F. Heat a cast-iron casserole over medium to high heat. When hot, spray or brush with oil and add shanks. Cook for 3–4 minutes each side or until golden. Remove and place on paper towels. You may have to do this in two batches, depending on the size of your casserole. Add a little more olive oil to casserole and add garlic and mushroom. Sauté for 1 minute. Add diced vegetables and cook for 4–5 minutes over medium heat, stirring regularly. Add wine and reduce slightly. Add tomatoes, stock and rosemary and stir. Place veal evenly in the sauce. If veal is not covered, add more stock. Bring to the boil. Remove from heat, cover and bake for 1½ hours. Remove lid and bake for a further ½ hour.

To serve, place mash in the middle of each plate. Mix salsa with shanks and ladle onto mash.

Note   As a time-saver, you can use a food processor to dice vegetables, but be careful not to overblend. Add a little extra oil to pan if mushrooms are sticking. This dish takes time to cook but is certainly worth the wait and little extra organization. As shanks are usually quite fatty, skim fat from dish once cooked. Better still make it the day before, refrigerate and remove solidified fat before reheating.

Variations   Use turkey or lamb shanks instead of veal. Any mash works beautifully with this favorite.

CHARGRILLED LAMB CUTLETS WITH TOMATO, CUCUMBER AND FETA

SERVES 4

prep time: 10 minutes

cook time: 5–10 minutes

12	**lamb loin cutlets**
	olive oil/olive oil spray
	sea salt
	cracked pepper
4	**handfuls fresh spinach**
4	**tablespoons *cucumber and mint yogurt sauce* (see page 163)**
	***tomato, cucumber and feta* (see page 131)**

Preheat barbecue or griddle pan to medium to high heat. Trim all visible fat from lamb, lightly brush or spray with oil and season with salt and pepper. When barbecue is hot, add lamb, cook for 2 minutes each side until medium rare, or longer according to taste.

To serve, place a handful of spinach in the middle of each plate and pile tomato, cucumber and feta salad on top. Arrange cutlets to sit on salad and dollop a tablespoon of yogurt sauce over the cutlets.

Variations   Use arugula instead of spinach, and tomato, bocconcini and basil salad (see page 132) instead of tomato, cucumber and feta. For a quick alternative, use low-fat tzatziki instead of the yogurt sauce.

🐾 *kid friendly* without spinach and served on a mash. Replace feta with a milder cheese like Cheddar or mozzarella.

LAMB CUTLETS WITH MINT AND CILANTRO CHUTNEY

SERVES 4

prep time: 20 minutes

cook time: 5–10 minutes

12	**lamb cutlets**
4	**vine-ripened tomatoes, cut in half horizontally**
	olive oil/olive oil spray
	sea salt
	cracked pepper
4	**tablespoons *mint and cilantro chutney* (see page 170)**

Preheat barbecue or griddle pan. Trim all visible fat from lamb. Lightly brush or spray lamb and tomatoes with oil and season with salt and pepper. When barbecue is hot, add lamb and tomatoes. Cook for 2 minutes each side until lamb is medium rare, or longer according to taste.

To serve, stack cutlets on top of each other, dollop with chutney and place tomatoes on the side.

Note   Arugula, pear and pan-toasted walnuts (see page 133) is the perfect accompaniment for this meal. See picture of this dish opposite page 122.

Variations   Use a dollop of roasted red pepper sauce (see page 161) instead of chutney or add cucumber and mint yogurt sauce (see page 163). Use any of the different salts instead of salt and pepper.

LAMB WITH PESTO, ROASTED ZUCCHINI AND PEPPERS AND BAKED BEETS

SERVES 2

prep time: 10 minutes

cook time: 50 minutes

4   **lamb loin steaks (about 3 ounces each)**
1   **tablespoon *basil pesto* (see page 162)**
    olive oil/olive oil spray
1   **beet, topped and tailed**
    ***roasted peppers and zucchini* (see page 148)**

Preheat oven to 425°F. Cut beet in half horizontally. Tightly wrap each half in foil and bake for 45–50 minutes. Remove any visible fat from steaks and spread finely with pesto. Heat barbecue or a non-stick griddle pan over medium to high heat. When hot, brush or spray grill with oil and add steaks. Cook for 2–3 minutes each side until medium rare, or longer according to taste. Allow meat to rest for 5–10 minutes.

To serve, slice beet horizontally into $^1/_3$-inch widths and place 2 large slices next to each other on each plate. Slice lamb into $^3/_4$-inch diagonals and stack on top of beet. Pile peppers and zucchini on top.

Variations   As a quick alternative serve with tomato, bocconcini and basil pesto (see page 132) instead of peppers and zucchini, and for a slightly different flavor use cucumber and mint yogurt sauce (see page 163) or low-fat tzatziki. If you don't have any pesto on hand, use herb salt, Cajun or Moroccan spices (see page 176) or a little sea salt and cracked pepper.

LAMB SHANKS WITH CREAMED SPINACH

SERVES 4

prep time: 10 minutes

cook time: 90–120 minutes

8	**lamb shanks (about 6 ounces each)**
	sea salt
	cracked pepper
1	**tablespoon olive oil**
2	**leeks, cut into ⅓-inch slices, or 2 red onions, sliced into fine wedges**
2	**stalks celery, finely chopped**
1	**carrot, finely chopped**
2	**tablespoons balsamic vinegar**
6	**anchovies**
1	**cup red wine**
4	**cups beef stock**
4	**cloves garlic, finely chopped**
3	**sprigs rosemary or oregano**
	creamed spinach **(see page 141)**

Preheat oven to 350°F. Season drumsticks with salt and pepper. Heat a large cast-iron casserole over medium to high heat. When hot, add oil and cook drumsticks until golden all over. Remove drumsticks onto paper towels. You may have to do this in two batches. Add vegetables to casserole and reduce heat. Cook for 2–3 minutes, stirring regularly. Add balsamic vinegar, anchovies and red wine and reduce liquid slightly. Add stock, garlic and rosemary. Return drumsticks to casserole and bring to the boil. Remove from heat, cover and bake for 1½–2 hours.

To serve, spoon spinach into shallow soup bowls and ladle shanks and vegetables on top.

Note   When using lamb shanks, it's better to allow them to cool after cooking so that you can remove excess fat once solidified and reduce the amount of saturated fat in the dish.

Variations   Vegetable or chicken stock can be easily substituted in this recipe. Add 1 cup cooked or canned cannellini beans for a higher-carbohydrate but delicious alternative. Use 1 celeriac trimmed at the top and base and chopped into ¾-inch cubes instead of celery. Serve with herb-salted turnip chips (see page 151).

LAMB, EGGPLANT AND FETA WITH ROASTED RED PEPPER SAUCE

SERVES 2

prep time: 5 minutes

cook time: 30 minutes

1   eggplant, cut vertically into ⅓-inch slices
     olive oil/olive oil spray
     sea salt
4   lamb loin steaks (about 3 ounces each)
2   handfuls arugula or spinach
4   tablespoons low-fat feta marinated in oil
4   tablespoons *roasted red pepper sauce* (see page 161)
2   tablespoons basil, roughly chopped
     cracked pepper

Preheat oven to 450°F. Place eggplant on a non-stick tray or tray lined with parchment paper. Spray eggplant with oil and sprinkle with salt. Bake eggplant for about 20–25 minutes. Remove any visible fat from steaks. Brush or spray lamb with a little olive oil and season with salt and pepper. Heat barbecue or a non-stick griddle pan over medium to high heat. When hot, add steaks and cook for 2–3 minutes each side until medium rare, or longer according to taste. Remove from heat, cover and allow to rest for about 5 minutes.

To serve, overlap 4 slices of eggplant to make a square and place a handful of arugula on top. Cut lamb into thick slices and stack over arugula. Crumble feta on top, dollop with sauce and sprinkle with basil. Season to taste.

Note   You will only need 4 slices of eggplant, so keep leftovers for a snack or lunch the next day. See picture of this dish opposite page 170.

Variations   Use herb salt to season the meat. For a quick alternative replace eggplant with 2 large field mushrooms, brushed or sprayed with olive oil and barbecued. This recipe is also delicious with spicy red pepper chutney (see page 169) or avocado mash (see page 173).

RIB CHOPS IN TERIYAKI AND TOMATO ON CELERIAC MASH

SERVES 4

prep time: 10 minutes

cook time: 60 minutes

12	lamb rib chops or 8 chops		cracked pepper
1	tablespoon olive oil		*celeriac mash* (see page 153, variation)
2	carrots, roughly chopped		
1	red onion, chopped into small wedges, retaining base		**Teriyaki and Tomato Marinade**
4	stalks celery or ½ medium fennel, roughly chopped	2	tablespoons tomato paste
		2	tablespoons teriyaki sauce
2	cups beef stock	1	teaspoon Worcestershire sauce
1	pound canned crushed tomatoes	1	tablespoon lemon juice
	sea salt	¼	cup verjuice

Preheat oven to 400°F. Trim all visible fat from lamb. Prepare marinade by combining tomato paste, teriyaki sauce, Worcestershire sauce, lemon juice and verjuice. Marinate lamb for at least 15 minutes and overnight if possible. Heat a heavy cast-iron casserole over medium to high heat. Remove lamb from marinade and retain liquid. Add lamb to casserole and cook for 1–2 minutes each side. Remove and place on paper towels. Add oil to casserole and cook vegetables for 3–4 minutes, stirring regularly. Add stock, tomatoes and marinade and return lamb to pot. Bring to the boil. Season to taste. Remove from heat, cover and bake for 45 minutes to 1 hour.

To serve, place mash on each plate and ladle lamb and vegetables over mash.

Variations　A simple green salad or lightly steamed sugar snaps instead of mash are different low-carbohydrate alternatives, or serve lamb on a bed of shredded cabbage (see page 110). When celeriac is unavailable serve with cauliflower mash (see page 153) or broccoli and parsnip mash (see page 155). For extra flavor, add 4 tablespoons parsley and lemon salsa, a variation of cilantro, parsley and lemon salsa (see page 172).

🦂 *kid friendly* on a mash or with chips.

MINI LAMB ROAST WITH ROASTED VEGETABLES

SERVES 4

prep time: 25 minutes

cook time: 50 minutes

2   **mini lamb roasts, boned and trimmed (12–14 ounces each)**
1   **cup water**
    a good splash of red wine
    roasted vegetables with rosemary and garlic **(see page 147)**

Mustard and Parsley Coating
2   **tablespoons freshly chopped flat-leaf parsley**
2   **cloves garlic, finely chopped**
2   **tablespoons freshly chopped rosemary**
3   **tablespoons Dijon mustard**
1   **tablespoon olive oil**
1   **tablespoon light soy or balsamic vinegar**

Preheat oven to 400°F. Combine herbs with mustard, olive oil and soy and mix well. Coat lamb with mixture. Place lamb on a wire rack in a roasting pan and add water to the pan. Place lamb in oven and bake for 45 minutes until medium rare, or longer according to taste. Remove lamb when cooked, cover and leave to rest for 10–15 minutes. Meanwhile, in a saucepan combine juices from tray and red wine. Bring to the boil, then reduce heat and simmer.

To serve, slice meat into $1/3$-inch widths and place on a large platter. Scatter vegetables around meat and serve juices in a pitcher.

Note   Try to have the lamb as close to room temperature as possible before cooking. If you're roasting the vegetables with the lamb, you may need to cook them a little longer than suggested in the recipe on page 147, as the oven here is not as hot.

Variations   Simply sprinkle lamb with herb salt and brush or spray with olive oil or spread some pesto over lamb instead of mustard and parsley coating. Delicious with pumpkin or sweet potato mash (see page 154) and wilted or creamed spinach (see page 141) with parsnip chips (see page 151, variation of herb-salted turnip chips).

🌼 *kid friendly* Most kids love a roast and this is no exception. Remove coating if they are fussy about "green bits" and add some cubed potatoes (with skins on) to the roast veggies.

PORK STEAKS IN ORANGE AND GINGER WITH BUTTON MUSHROOMS

SERVES 4

prep time: 10 minutes

cook time: 10 minutes

¾	cup freshly squeezed orange juice (about 2 oranges)
1	teaspoon freshly grated ginger
1	tablespoon light soy
1	teaspoon sesame oil
4	pork loin steaks
	olive oil/olive oil spray
8	ounces button mushrooms, halved
4	heads broccolini

Mix orange juice, ginger, soy and oil in a glass bowl and marinate pork for at least 1 hour. The flavors of this dish improve if pork is allowed to marinate overnight. Heat a large non-stick frying pan over medium heat. When hot, brush or spray with oil. Remove steaks from marinade and add to pan with mushrooms for 2 minutes each side or until just cooked. Remove pork and keep warm. The meat will continue to cook once taken off the heat. Meanwhile steam broccolini until just cooked and still crisp, about 4–5 minutes. Add marinade to mushrooms in pan and bring to the boil. Remove from heat and serve.

To serve, stack broccolini to the side of plate and place pork in the center. Spoon over mushrooms and marinade.

Note   Try to have the pork as close to room temperature as possible before cooking.

Variation   Use broccoli if you're unable to find broccolini.

Opposite: Lamb Cutlets with Mint and Cilantro Chutney (page 116) with Arugula, Pear and Pan-toasted Walnuts (page 133)

PORK STEAKS WITH PESTO WRAPPED IN PROSCIUTTO

SERVES 4

prep time: 15 minutes

cook time: 20 minutes

4   **ounces pork butterfly steaks (about 6 ounces each)**
2   **teaspoons *basil pesto* (see page 162)**
1   **cup baby spinach (loosely packed)**
4   **tablespoons grated light mozzarella**
4   **slices prosciutto, sliced lengthwise into equal halves**
     cracked pepper
     olive oil spray
     sea salt

Preheat oven to 350°F. Spread $^{1}/_{2}$-teaspoon pesto on one half of pork steak. Layer spinach leaves on top of pesto and sprinkle with mozzarella. Fold other half of pork over cheese and wrap a piece of prosciutto around each steak to secure filling. Tuck ends under. Wrap the second slice across the steak to form a cross and again tuck ends under. Spray with olive oil and season with salt and pepper. Place in a non-stick baking dish or dish lined with parchment paper and bake for 20 minutes or until cooked to your liking.

To serve, place pork on each plate and serve with a simple green salad.

Variations   Replace pesto with fresh sage or thyme and spread a thin layer of goat cheese marinated in oil instead of mozzarella. You could also serve each pork parcel on a bed of wilted spinach with roasted tomato sauce dolloped on top or roasted peppers and zucchini.

Opposite: Coriander-Crusted Beef (page 101) with Green Beans and Sweet Potato and Ginger Mash (page 154, variation)

PORK CHOPS IN MUSTARD AND LEMON WITH TOMATO

SERVES 4

prep time: 5 minutes

cook time: 10 minutes

4	**midloin pork chops, trimmed**
1	**pound asparagus**
	olive oil/olive oil spray
3	**ripe tomatoes, cut into ¾-inch slices**
	mustard, lemon and verjuice marinade (see page 175)

Add pork to marinade for at least 15 minutes and longer if possible. Snap ends off asparagus where they break naturally. Heat a non-stick griddle pan or frying pan over medium to low heat. When hot, brush or spray with olive oil. Add chops and tomato to pan. Cook for 3–4 minutes each side or according to taste and drizzle a little marinade over tomato. Meanwhile lightly steam asparagus until just cooked and still crisp, about 2–3 minutes. Remove and plunge into cold water. Remove pork and tomato to a plate and add remaining marinade to pan. Bring to the boil, then remove from heat.

To serve, position pork on each plate, with tomatoes on top and asparagus (heads together) alongside. Drizzle remaining marinade over pork.

Note   The chops may take a few minutes longer than the tomatoes, so stack slices on top of each other and move to edge of pan.

Variations   When asparagus is unavailable use beans or a simple green salad. Serve chops on a bed of sauerkraut – a wonderful low-carb dish that is delicious with pork and beef and is believed to improve nutrient absorption and help digestion. Simply place 4 cups sauerkraut in a saucepan with 1 cup chicken stock. Bring to the boil then simmer for 15 minutes. Add 1 tablespoon dijonnaise or, for a more natural and lower-fat option, 1 teaspoon Dijon mustard and 2 teaspoons low-fat mayonnaise or light sour cream.

TARRAGON PORK WITH VERJUICE AND PEACH

SERVES 4

prep time: 10 minutes

cook time: 35 minutes

2	**tablespoons tarragon, finely chopped**
1	**teaspoon sea salt**
	cracked pepper
1½	**pounds pork tenderloin**
	olive oil/olive oil spray
1	**tablespoon butter**
½	**savoy cabbage, finely sliced**
2	**ripe peaches, each sliced into 8 wedges**
½	**cup verjuice (see page 175)**
½	**cup chicken stock**

Preheat oven to 350°F. Mix tarragon with salt and cracked pepper on a cutting board. Roll both sides of pork firmly across herb mixture. Heat a large non-stick frying pan over medium to high heat. When hot, spray or brush with olive oil and add pork. Cook for 3 minutes each side or until golden. Remove from pan and place on a non-stick tray or tray lined with parchment paper. Bake for 25–30 minutes. Remove and keep warm. Allow meat to rest for 10 minutes. Place a large saucepan over medium heat and add butter. When butter starts to sizzle, add cabbage and a pinch of salt. Cook cabbage for 5–10 minutes or until softened. Remove from heat and cover. Wipe frying pan clean and spray or brush with olive oil and add peaches. Cook for 1–2 minutes each side over medium to low heat or until golden and softened. Add verjuice and chicken stock and bring to the boil. Remove from heat and serve.

To serve, cut pork into $^3/_4$-inch slices. Place cabbage in center of each plate with pork slices on top. Spoon over peaches and drizzle with sauce.

Note   Use canned or bottled peaches or a large green apple, peeled and finely sliced, when fresh peaches are unavailable. See picture of this dish opposite page 106.

Variations   Serve with pumpkin and ginger mash (see page 154), although the carbohydrate content is slightly higher. Replace $^1/_2$ savoy cabbage with 12 handfuls spinach, $^1/_2$ red cabbage or 4 cups sauerkraut. Cook finely sliced red cabbage or sauerkraut with 1 cup chicken stock for 15 minutes, covered, then add butter. (Also see sauerkraut variation in pork chops in mustard and lemon, page 124.)

kid friendly on broccoli and parsnip mash (see page 155).

PORK AND LIME STIRFRY WITH EGGPLANT AND RED PEPPER

SERVES 4

prep time: 10 minutes

cook time: 12 minutes

1–2	tablespoons sesame oil
1	eggplant, cut into large cubes
2	whole cloves garlic, squashed
1	bunch cilantro leaves, roughly chopped, with roots and stems scraped and finely chopped
4	kaffir lime leaves, finely sliced
1	pound ground pork
1	tablespoon fish sauce
2	tablespoons light soy
2	tablespoons lime juice
1	red pepper, cut into thin slices
½	iceberg lettuce

Heat a large non-stick wok or frying pan over medium to high heat. When hot, spray or brush well with oil and add eggplant. Cook for 5–6 minutes or until golden and cooked through, shaking regularly. Remove eggplant and place on kitchen paper. Return wok to medium to high heat and when hot, add a little more oil, garlic, cilantro roots and stems and lime leaves and cook for 1 minute. Remove garlic and discard. Add pork and cook for 2–3 minutes. Add fish sauce, soy and lime juice and stir. Add pepper and cook for 1–2 minutes. Return eggplant to wok and toss gently. Add cilantro leaves, mix well and remove from heat.

To serve, make lettuce cups by carefully peeling off whole lettuce leaves and serve at the table by spooning pork into lettuce cups.

Note   Use lemon leaves if lime leaves are unavailable. Adding cilantro root is optional as it entails more work, but it's definitely worthwhile for the intensity of the flavor.

Variation   For a spicy hit add a small seeded, chopped chile and 2 finely sliced lemongrass stems to the wok when you add garlic and lime leaves.

MINI PORK BURGERS ON BRAISED CABBAGE AND APPLE

SERVES 4

prep time: 15 minutes

cook time: 10 minutes

2	**leeks**
1	**pound lean ground pork**
2	**cloves garlic**
2	**handfuls basil**
2	**tablespoons almond meal**
1	**egg**
4	**sun-dried tomatoes**
2	**tablespoons tomato paste**
	good pinch of salt
4	**tablespoons shredded Parmesan**
	olive oil/olive oil spray
	***braised red cabbage and apple* (see page 142)**
	***roasted tomato sauce* (see page 160)**

Steam or microwave leeks until softened, then blend or process with pork, garlic, basil, almond meal, egg, sun-dried tomatoes, tomato paste and salt. When combined, mix with Parmesan. Roll mixture into burgers the size of a golf ball, cover and refrigerate. To cook burgers, heat a large non-stick griddle pan or frying pan over medium to low heat. When hot, brush or spray with olive oil. Cook for 2–3 minutes each side or until cooked through and golden.

To serve, place cabbage on each plate with burgers on top and dollop with sauce.

Variations   Serve with low-fat tzatziki instead of tomato sauce. The burgers are delicious immersed in roasted tomato sauce and sprinkled with Parmesan. Ground chicken works equally well in this recipe.

🌼 *kid friendly* without cabbage, served on noodles with roasted tomato sauce and shredded Parmesan.

SIDE SALADS and VEGETABLES

As a low-fat, high-carb eater of the eighties, I usually sacrificed vegetables and salads for rice,

pasta and potatoes. Vegetables disappeared into my pasta sauce and a green salad was squeezed

in only after a second helping of rigatoni matriciana. Now, many vegetables have taken on a new life

in the search for substitutes for old favorites; comfort foods such as mash, fries and roast vegetables

are still on the menu but with a few interesting twists. Salads and vegetables make fabulous starters.

Try the fennel in Parmesan and almond or the different vegetable stacks – simply served as is or

placed on a bed of roasted tomato sauce. When roasting, steaming or sautéing you can cook

vegetables for more than just one meal. They make excellent snacks or an instant lunch the next day.

Simply team them with some lean protein: shredded turkey, chicken or canned fish. When the meat

or protein source requires a bit of work, keep the vegetables simple. Similarly, if you are just grilling

a piece of meat or steaming fish, you can make a little extra effort with the side dishes.

(It is a good idea to include plenty of raw vegetables in your diet. Although vegetables contain relatively low levels of protein, heat from cooking does damage important enzymes.)

Salad greens are nutritiously dense and low in carbohydrates and fat. They are excellent to pad out a dish and decrease the carbohydrate density of side dishes containing pumpkin, sweet potato or legumes.and beans. Any meal can be accompanied by a simple green salad. To serve 4 people, take 6 large handfuls of any lettuce – iceberg, arugula, endive, watercress, butter, leaf, romaine or a mixture – or slice baby romaine in half or cut an iceberg lettuce into wedges. Dress it with 2 tablespoons of dressing – balsamic and garlic, Thai lime, lemon Caesar or simply good olive oil or flaxseed oil and a little balsamic, red or white wine vinegar or lemon juice with a sprinkle of sea salt and cracked pepper. The dressing you choose should complement the flavors of the meal. For variations, add a combination of fresh herbs and/or any green vegetables and some nuts or seeds.

Play with colors and textures and enjoy not just the smell and taste but the presentation of salads and vegetables.

CUCUMBER WITH YOGURT AND LIME

SERVES 4

prep time: 5 minutes

1   **English cucumber**
     yogurt and lime dressing (see page 166)

Finely slice cucumber into long, thin, flat strips or finely chop. Add to dressing and gently mix.
Serve with fish, lamb or chicken.

Variations   Combine 2 seeded and finely chopped tomatoes and a handful of chopped cilantro and drizzle
with Chinese soy and sesame dressing instead of yogurt and lime dressing. For something different, add
$1/2$-cup chopped honeydew melon to the salad. Low-fat tzatziki with lime juice is a good, quick alternative
to yogurt and lime dressing.

TOMATO, CUCUMBER AND FETA

prep time: 5 minutes

3	vine-ripened tomatoes, cut into ¾-inch cubes
2	English cucumbers, cut into ¾-inch cubes
½	cup low-fat feta, crumbled
12	kalamata olives, pitted and sliced
1	handful flat-leaf parsley, roughly chopped
	drizzle of extra virgin olive oil or flaxseed oil (optional)
	cracked pepper
	sea salt

Mix together all ingredients, and season with salt and pepper to taste. Serve with lamb, beef and chicken.

Note   If you're using marinated feta or goat cheese, you will not need to include the extra drizzle of oil.

Variations   Finely slice ¼ red onion and use in addition to or instead of olives. Use basil instead of parsley or goat cheese instead of feta. For a visual difference, cut roma tomatoes into long segments, cucumber into long diagonals and red onion into wedges.

TOMATO, BOCCONCINI AND BASIL PESTO

SERVES 4

prep time: 5 minutes

1	**pint cherry tomatoes, halved**
1	**package baby bocconcini balls (about 8 ounces), halved**
2	**teaspoons *basil pesto* (see page 162)**
1	**handful freshly chopped basil**
	cracked pepper

Place tomato and bocconcini in a bowl with basil and add pesto. Gently mix and season with cracked pepper. Serve with lamb, chicken and beef.

Variations   Use cilantro or mint pesto for a change, leaving out basil and using cilantro or mint in the salad. Combine with roasted peppers and zucchini (see page 148) for a great antipasto salad.

ARUGULA, PEAR AND PAN-TOASTED WALNUTS

S E R V E S 4

prep time: 10 minutes

cook time: 2 minutes

1	**teaspoon butter**
1	**teaspoon olive oil**
1	**handful shelled walnut pieces (1¾ ounces)**
4	**tablespoons grated Parmesan**
	sea salt
4	**large handfuls arugula**
1	**Bosc pear, cut into fine segments**
3	**tablespoons *lemon Caesar dressing* (see page 165)**
	cracked pepper

Heat a non-stick frying pan over medium heat. Add butter and oil. Break walnuts into pieces and add to pan once butter has melted. Cook walnuts, shaking frequently, until golden. Scatter 1 tablespoon Parmesan over walnuts and remove from heat. Sprinkle walnuts with a little salt.

To serve, place arugula and pear on a large platter. Scatter over walnuts and drizzle with lemon Caesar dressing. Top with remaining Parmesan and cracked pepper. Serve with chicken, lamb, turkey, beef, pork, fish or frittata.

Note   Commercial Caesar salad dressing is a great time-saver and you can enhance its flavor by adding 1 tablespoon white wine vinegar or white balsamic and 1 tablespoon lemon juice to 3 tablespoons dressing. See picture of this dish opposite page 122.

Variations   Omit walnuts, dressing and Parmesan. Add 4 finely shredded Jerusalem artichokes or a finely sliced baby fennel, sprinkle with 2 tablespoons feta or goat cheese marinated in oil, drizzle with balsamic and a little oil from the cheese.

LOW-CARB ROASTED VEGETABLES

SERVES 4

prep time: 10 minutes

cook time: 35–40 minutes

1	cup pumpkin, cut into 1-inch cubes
1	eggplant, cut into 1-inch cubes
2	zucchini, cut into small batons
2	red onions, sliced into wedges with base intact
12	thick asparagus spears, cut into 2-inch lengths
	olive oil/olive oil spray
	sea salt
	cracked pepper
4	tablespoons marinated low-fat feta (about 1¾ ounces)
1	handful basil

Preheat oven to 425°F. Place all vegetables (except asparagus) on a roasting pan lined with parchment paper in a single layer. Spray or lightly brush with oil and lightly sprinkle with salt and pepper. Bake for 35–40 minutes or until golden. Add asparagus after 20 minutes and spray with oil.

Serve hot or cold and sprinkle with feta and basil just prior to serving.

Note   Try to cut vegetables to roughly the same size.

Variations   Use goat cheese marinated in oil or shredded Parmesan instead of feta. While vegetables are still warm, add 2 handfuls spinach and gently toss.

MINT TABBOULEH

SERVES 4

prep time: 30 minutes

¼   **cup bulgur (cracked wheat)**
1   **cup chicken stock or water**
2   **semi-dried tomatoes marinated in oil, finely sliced**
1   **English cucumber, diced**
2   **green onions, finely chopped**
2   **cups finely chopped flat-leaf parsley**
1   **cup finely chopped mint**
    zest and juice of 1 lemon
2   **vine-ripened tomatoes, seeded and diced**
1   **tablespoon virgin olive oil or flaxseed oil**
    sea salt
    cracked pepper

Place bulgur in a bowl and cover with chicken stock for 20–30 minutes. Place bulgur in a fine sieve and press with spoon to remove excess liquid. Spread bulgur on paper towels and pat dry. Combine bulgur, semi-dried tomatoes, cucumber, green onion, parsley and mint in a high-sided bowl. Squeeze lemon juice over salad. Scatter tomato on top. Drizzle with olive oil, sprinkle with lemon zest and season with salt and pepper. Serve with beef, lamb or chicken and top with either avocado mash (see page 173) or cucumber and mint yogurt sauce (see page 163).

Note   Bulgur or cracked wheat is a good source of dietary fiber and B vitamins. Fiber helps to prevent constipation and hemorrhoids and may even reduce the risk of bowel cancer. See picture of this dish opposite page 138.

CHINESE CABBAGE, SHREDDED BEETS AND CASHEWS

prep time: 10–15 minutes

3	tablespoons cashews or slivered almonds
3	cups Chinese cabbage, finely sliced
1	handful cilantro
1	handful finely chopped mint
1	red pepper, sliced into thin strips
1	handful bean sprouts and snow pea sprouts
1	beet, finely shredded
1	cup snow peas, finely shredded
4–6	tablespoons *Chinese soy and sesame dressing* (see page 165)

Preheat oven to 400°F. Crush cashews and place on a non-stick tray or tray lined with parchment paper and bake for 5–10 minutes or until golden. Place all ingredients in a large bowl. Drizzle dressing over salad, mixing well. Serve with grilled fish, chicken, lamb or beef.

Note   Most processors have a shredding component, but hand-held shredders or julienne cutters take seconds to use and wash. Try to dress salad 1 hour before serving for a really intense flavor.

Variations   Use Thai lime dressing (see page 164) and add finely sliced chicken, lamb or beef to make a complete meal. Substitute snow peas for 1 finely shredded carrot.

NECTARINE, GOAT CHEESE AND PANCETTA

SERVES 2

prep time: 7–10 minutes

cook time: 5 minutes

4   **slices pancetta or 2 slices prosciutto (about 1½ ounces)**
1   **nectarine, sliced into fine segments**
1   **handful mint, roughly torn**
2   **handfuls green oakleaf, butter or leaf lettuce or arugula**
2   **tablespoons goat cheese marinated in oil**
1   **tablespoon virgin olive oil or olive oil from the goat cheese**
2   **teaspoons lemon juice**
    sea salt
    cracked pepper

Heat a non-stick frying pan over medium heat and cook pancetta for 1–2 minutes each side or until crisp. Mix nectarine, mint and pancetta with lettuce and crumble goat cheese over the top. Drizzle oil and squeeze lemon over salad. Season with salt and pepper. Serve with chicken, fish or lamb.

Note   Don't be put off by the goat cheese – this is a very mild, creamy and divine cheese.

Variations   Try 10 bocconcini balls cut into quarters or marinated low-fat feta instead of goat cheese. Use a ripe peach or 2 ripe figs instead of a nectarine or add ¼ red onion and avocado, finely sliced. For a lower-carbohydrate option, forget the fruit and use 1 chopped vine-ripened tomato. Shred 2 cooked chicken breasts and toss through salad for a complete meal.

WATERCRESS, ROASTED PUMPKIN AND PROSCIUTTO

SERVES 4

prep time: 10 minutes

cook time: 30 minutes

4	**ounces pumpkin, cut into 1-inch cubes**
	olive oil spray
	sea salt
2	**tablespoons pistachio nuts, shelled**
4	**slices prosciutto, roughly torn**
3	**handfuls butter, leaf or green oakleaf lettuce**
1	**handful watercress**
¼	**red onion, finely sliced**
2	**tablespoons *balsamic and garlic dressing* (see page 166)**
	cracked pepper

Preheat oven to 425°F. Place pumpkin on a tray lined with parchment paper and lightly spray with oil. Sprinkle with salt and bake for 30 minutes or until golden. Meanwhile bake pistachios for 10–15 minutes and prosciutto for 4–5 minutes or until crisp and golden.

To serve, place all ingredients in a bowl, drizzle with dressing and season with cracked pepper. Mix well. Serve with chicken, turkey breast, pork, lamb or beef.

Variations   Replace watercress with a bunch of asparagus (about 10½ ounces) or arugula. For extra texture and flavor, add shaved Parmesan or crumble a little marinated goat cheese over the top and drizzle with its own oil and a little balsamic or lemon juice.

Opposite: Mint Tabbouleh (page 135)

BALSAMIC TOMATOES

SERVES 2

prep time: 1 minute

cook time: 5 minutes

olive oil/olive oil spray
2   tomatoes, halved
balsamic vinegar
1   tablespoon basil (optional), finely sliced

Heat a non-stick griddle or frying pan over medium heat. When hot, brush or spray with oil. Add tomato cut-side up and drizzle with balsamic vinegar. Cook for 2 minutes each side. Scatter basil over tomato. Serve with chicken, turkey, pork, veal, lamb or beef.

Variations   Spread a little pesto over each tomato or sprinkle with a little shaved Parmesan.

Opposite: Veal Rack with Fennel and Broad Beans (page 113)

SAUTÉED MUSHROOMS AND GARLIC

SERVES 2

prep time: 5 minutes

cook time: 5 minutes

2   **teaspoons butter or olive oil**

1   **clove garlic, finely chopped**

8   **ounces brown, flat or field mushrooms, finely chopped**

1   **handful flat-leaf parsley (optional), finely chopped**

Heat a non-stick frying pan over medium to high heat. Add butter and garlic and cook for 1 minute. Add mushrooms and parsley and cook for a further 2–3 minutes, stirring regularly. Serve as bed for chicken, turkey, veal, lamb or beef. Dollop on top of some protein, spoon into an omelet or scatter over a poached egg.

Variations   Slice mushrooms rather than chop and add a couple of handfuls of arugula or spinach to pan for 1 minute once mushrooms are cooked.

CREAMED SPINACH

SERVES 2

prep time: 1 minute

cook time: 5 minutes

8   **handfuls spinach**

1   **tablespoon water**

2   **tablespoons low-fat ricotta**

    pinch of sea salt

Heat a large saucepan over medium heat. Add spinach and water, cook for 2 minutes or until spinach has wilted. Remove from heat and add ricotta and salt. Blend until combined. Serve as a bed for lamb, beef, fish, chicken, turkey, pork or veal or add a few tablespoons to an omelet or frittata.

Note   Spinach is an excellent source of carotenoids, which is a vitamin A fat-soluble vitamin and has antioxidant qualities. It is a good source of vitamin C and is considered to be one of the most powerful vegetables in preventing cancer. Spinach also contains iron and folate to protect and assist in the development of the nervous system.

Variations   Add nutmeg, garlic or occasionally substitute ricotta for cream or 2 teaspoons of butter for an extra creamy dish – and extra saturated fat! Use a bunch of Swiss chard (discarding stalks) instead of spinach.

BRAISED RED CABBAGE AND APPLE

SERVES 2

prep time: 5 minutes

cook time: 25 minutes

¼   **large head red cabbage or ¼ savoy cabbage**
1   **tablespoon butter or olive oil**
½   **green apple, peeled and shredded**
½   **cup chicken stock**
1   **teaspoon whole-grain French mustard**

Finely slice cabbage and discard core. Melt butter in a non-stick frying pan over medium heat. Add cabbage when butter is foaming. Cook cabbage for 5 minutes, stirring regularly, or until it begins to wilt. Add apple and stir. When mixture begins to caramelize, add stock and mustard. Reduce heat and simmer for approximately 10 minutes, adding more stock if cabbage starts to dry out. Serve as a bed for pork, turkey or chicken.

Note   Cabbage is not only an excellent source of vitamin C, but is thought to prevent colon cancer, relieve gastric ulcers and may help to prevent breast and ovarian cancer in women.

Variation   Replace cabbage with ½ large fennel finely sliced and cut apple into fine segments instead of shredding.

EGGPLANT, RED PEPPER AND OLIVES

SERVES 4

prep time: 7 minutes

cook time: 65 minutes

1	tablespoon olive oil
2	cloves garlic, cut into slivers
1	pound canned peeled, diced tomatoes
	pinch of sea salt
2	red peppers, chopped into ¾-inch cubes
1	eggplant, chopped into ¾-inch cubes
12	kalamata olives
1	handful basil

Heat a cast-iron saucepan over medium heat. When hot, add oil and garlic. Cook garlic until softened but do not brown. Add tomatoes and salt. Simmer for 5 minutes. Add pepper and eggplant to tomatoes. Reduce heat and simmer for about 1 hour. Add a handful of chopped basil and olives. Stir and cook for a minute longer and serve. Serve as a bed or sauce for pork, veal, chicken, lamb, fish or sautéed tofu.

Note   This takes a little longer to cook than most dishes but it is extremely versatile. Double the quantity and freeze the excess. This is a variation on my Irish girlfriend's delicious repertoire.

Variation   Add 4 chopped anchovy fillets with tomatoes and forget the salt.

FENNEL IN PARMESAN AND ALMOND

SERVES 4

prep time: 5 minutes

cook time: 5 minutes

1	**large fennel**
¼	**cup grated Parmesan**
¼	**cup almond meal**
	sea salt
	cracked pepper
1	**egg**
1	**tablespoon olive oil**
	extra Parmesan

Remove outer leaves of fennel and trim stalks 2 inches or so from top of bulb. Retaining base, cut fennel in half lengthwise and each half into finger-width slices. Retain fennel leaves and roughly chop.

Combine ¼-cup Parmesan with almond meal. Season with salt and pepper. Lightly beat egg and dip fennel slices in egg, then press Parmesan and almond meal mixture onto fennel. Heat a large non-stick frying pan over medium heat. When hot, add oil and fennel slices. Cook for 2 minutes each side or until coating is golden.

To serve, sprinkle with extra Parmesan and chopped fennel leaves and drizzle with a little olive oil. Excellent with beef, chicken, lamb or fish or on a bed of roasted tomato sauce (see page 160) or a handful of arugula as a starter, for lunch or light supper.

Variation A little truffle oil is delicious drizzled over the finished product.

SIMPLE GREEN VEGETABLES

SERVES 4

prep time: 5 minutes

cook time: 5 minutes

¼   **cup water**

4   **handfuls snow peas or green beans or asparagus or broccolini**

4   **baby bok choy or 8 handfuls baby spinach or arugula or**
    1 bunch choy sum or similar leaf vegetable, roughly chopped

Place a wok or large non-stick frying pan over medium to high heat. Add water, cover and bring to the boil. Add your choice of snow peas, green beans, asparagus or broccolini and cook for 1–2 minutes, covered. Add your choice of leaves and cook for 1–2 minutes more with the lid on. Keep checking water level and add a little more water to avoid vegetables sticking. Gently toss greens while cooking. Remove greens and serve immediately.

Note   If using the variations and returning vegetables to wok or pan it is better to undercook the vegetables initially.

Variations   After braising vegetables, gently remove. Place a wok or large non-stick frying pan over medium to high heat. When hot, add 1 tablespoon olive oil and 2 finely sliced garlic cloves and cook for a few seconds. Return wilted greens to wok and gently toss. Sprinkle with 2 tablespoons shaved Parmesan and serve on a large platter. Instead of adding olive oil and sliced garlic, add 1 tablespoon sesame oil, 1 tablespoon shredded ginger and 1 teaspoon sambal oelek (chile paste). Cook for a few seconds and return wilted greens to wok. Gently toss, adding 1 tablespoon light soy and 1 tablespoon toasted sesame seeds. The variations for this side dish are endless – consider adding slivered almonds, hazelnuts or cashews together with various fresh herbs such as cilantro, basil or flat-leaf parsley. Keep the flavors simple and clean and, again, make sure they complement the main dish.

ROASTED BEETS AND RED ONION

SERVES 4

prep time: 5 minutes

cook time: 50 minutes

4	**beets**
2	**red onions**
	olive oil/olive oil spray
1	**tablespoon balsamic vinegar**
	sea salt

Preheat oven to 425°F. Wash beets thoroughly and scrub. Trim tops, leaving a $^3/_4$-inch stalk. Cut beets and onion into 8 segments, retaining base of onion. Place on a non-stick tray or tray lined with baking paper. Spray or brush with oil, drizzle with balsamic vinegar and season generously with salt. Bake for 45–50 minutes or until cooked. Toss together and serve with beef, lamb, chicken, turkey or pork.

Note   Beets will stain your fingers temporarily so beware or wear kitchen gloves.

Variations   Add a large fennel sliced into wedges and bake with onion and beet or toss 2 handfuls lightly steamed beans or asparagus with vegetables once cooked. Keep the tail of the beans intact.

ROASTED VEGETABLES WITH ROSEMARY AND GARLIC

SERVES 4

prep time: 10 minutes

cook time: 45–50 minutes

1   red pepper, chopped into ¾-inch squares

4   baby carrots, chopped into ¾-inch squares

1   cup pumpkin or sweet potato, chopped into ¾-inch squares

1   red onion, sliced into wedges, retaining base

1   celeriac, peeled and chopped into ¾-inch squares

2   zucchini, chopped into ¾-inch squares

6   cloves garlic, smashed
     olive oil/olive oil spray
     sea salt

4   sprigs rosemary

Preheat oven to 425°F. Place all vegetables in a single layer on a non-sick tray or tray lined with parchment paper. Toss garlic with vegetables and spray or brush well with oil and season with salt. Tear rosemary sprigs into small pieces, scatter over vegetables and gently toss. Bake for 45–50 minutes or until golden. Toss every 15 minutes. Remove zucchini and red onion after about 40 minutes and keep warm. They will be cooked before other vegetables.

Serve as a bed for lamb or with any lean roast of beef, chicken, turkey, veal or pork. If cooking for 2, keep leftovers and combine with cold chicken, turkey, lamb or beef, a handful of salad greens and some olive oil and balsamic, red or white wine vinegar for lunch the next day.

Note   Do not peel vegetables (except celeriac), so as to retain as many vitamins and minerals and as much fiber as possible.

ROASTED PEPPERS AND ZUCCHINI

SERVES 4

prep time: 10 minutes

cook time: 30 minutes

3   **zucchini**

1   **red pepper**

1   **yellow pepper**

1   **green pepper**

     sea salt

     cracked pepper

     olive oil/olive oil spray

Preheat oven to 425°F. Cut zucchini and peppers in half lengthwise and remove seeds and pith from peppers. Place zucchini and peppers cut-side down on a non-stick baking tray or tray lined with parchment paper. Lightly brush or spray zucchini with oil and sprinkle with a little salt. Bake vegetables for 25–30 minutes or until peppers blister and darken and zucchini is golden.

Place peppers in plastic bag for 10 minutes. Meanwhile slice zucchini into slices. Remove peppers from bag and peel. Slice peppers into strips. Gently mix peppers and zucchini together. Serve warm with lamb, chicken, turkey or beef.

Variation   Serve cold as salad or on an antipasto platter and drizzle a little balsamic vinegar and scatter a handful of finely chopped basil or mint on top.

ROASTED EGGPLANT WITH MIRIN AND SESAME SEEDS

prep time: 5 minutes

cook time: 40 minutes

1	**eggplant**
1	**tablespoon freshly grated ginger**
1	**tablespoon sesame oil**

Sauce

2	**tablespoons soy**
1	**teaspoon white miso paste**
1	**tablespoon mirin**
2	**teaspoons sesame seeds**

Preheat oven to 425°F. Cut eggplant in half lengthwise. Score each half with deep diagonal cuts. Mix ginger with sesame oil. Spread over top of eggplant. Place on a non-stick baking tray or tray lined with parchment paper and bake for 30 minutes. Meanwhile mix together all ingredients for sauce. When eggplant is cooked, remove from oven and pour sauce evenly over eggplant. Return to oven and bake for 5–10 minutes more. Serve as a starter or with a simple spinach salad as a light supper.

Note   Mirin is not a low-carb condiment so you may want to reduce the amount used or avoid the dish entirely.

MUSHROOM, SPINACH AND PARMESAN STACK

SERVES 2

prep time: 5 minutes

cook time: 30 minutes

2	large field, flat or portobello mushrooms
8	baby spinach leaves
2	tablespoons basil, finely sliced
2	tablespoons shredded Parmesan
1	ripe tomato, cut into ¾-inch cubes or slices
	olive oil/olive oil spray

Preheat oven to 425°F. Remove mushroom stalks and place mushrooms flesh-side up on a tray lined with baking paper. Place 4 spinach leaves inside mushroom and sprinkle with a little basil and then Parmesan. Place tomato on top and sprinkle with remaining basil and more Parmesan. Lightly brush or spray with oil and bake for 30 minutes or until cooked. Serve with fish, beef, lamb, veal, chicken or turkey.

Note   Use a large cooked mushroom as a bed for the protein component of your meal.

Variations   Simply stuff mushroom with a mixture of fresh herbs, almond meal or crushed walnuts or sunflower seeds, butter, salt and pepper. Spread with pesto or drizzle with truffle oil and sprinkle with crushed garlic and herb salt. Replace basil with thyme or oregano and Parmesan with goat cheese, mozzarella or bocconcini.

HERB-SALTED TURNIP CHIPS

SERVES 4

prep time: 5 minutes

cook time: 25 minutes

4   **turnips**
     herb salt
     olive oil spray

Preheat oven to 425°F. Slice bottoms of turnips and cut into $^1/_4$- to $^3/_8$-inch slices. Place in a single layer on a tray lined with parchment paper. Spray well with oil and sprinkle with a little herb salt. Place in oven and bake for 20–25 minutes, turning chips after 10 minutes. Serve with fish, beef, lamb, turkey or chicken or as nibbles with pre-dinner drinks. Serve with dips, spicy roasted red pepper sauce, pesto mayonnaise or red pepper mayonnaise (see chapter 7).

Note   See photo of this dish and sweet potato chips opposite page 154.

Variations   Use celeriac, parsnip or sweet potato. Chop into $^3/_4$-inch cubes or finely slice into disks using a wide vegetable peeler. Alternatively put thin slices of vegetables in a plastic bag. Add 2 cloves chopped garlic, a splash of oil and 2 tablespoons shredded Parmesan. Shake. One of my cooking pals, Scotty, prefers this dish with sweet potato. Excellent with any protein. Cooking times will vary depending on the vegetable.

🌸 *kid friendly* – particularly the parsnip variation.

CHARGRILLED LOW-CARB VEGETABLES

SERVES 4

prep time: 5 min

cook time: depends on the size and heat of your barbecue or grill

2	zucchini, cut lengthwise into $\frac{1}{3}$-inch slices
3	baby eggplant, cut in half lengthwise, or 1 large eggplant, cut into $\frac{1}{3}$-inch slices
4	large flat field or portobello mushrooms, stalks removed
1	red pepper, membrane removed
	olive oil/olive oil spray
	sea salt
8	large black olives, halved and pitted
1	handful flat-leaf parsley, roughly chopped

Heat barbecue, grill or griddle pan to medium. Spray or brush both sides of vegetables with oil and sprinkle with sea salt. When grill is hot, add vegetables and cook until tender. Turn vegetables, leaving golden "char" marks. Remove vegetables and sprinkle with olives and parsley. Serve with grilled or barbecued lamb, beef or chicken.

Note   You may have to cook this in several batches. Keep cooked vegetables warm if you are wanting to serve this dish hot.

Variations   Use herb salt instead of sea salt. Allow to cool, drizzle with a little balsamic vinegar and sprinkle with chopped basil or flat-leaf parsley. Serve cold as a side salad and place vegetables on a bed of baby spinach or arugula, or serve as part of an antipasto platter.

CAULIFLOWER MASH WITH HORSERADISH CREAM

SERVES 4

prep time: 5 minutes

cook time: 15 minutes

1   ripe head cauliflower (about 1½-pounds)
¼   cup chicken stock
2   teaspoons butter
1   tablespoon horseradish cream (see page 167)
    salt

Roughly chop cauliflower and microwave in chicken stock or steam until very soft, about 10 minutes. Strain, retaining stock. Blend or process and add butter, horseradish cream and salt to taste. Add a little more stock if required.

Note   Mash is an extremely versatile side dish and with a few subtle changes in the vegetables and seasoning it will totally transform a dish. Cooking times will vary depending on whether you steam or microwave your vegetables. The make and model of your microwave will also significantly affect cooking times. Cauliflower, like broccoli, brussels sprouts and cabbage, is a cruciferous vegetable and contains a substance called "indoles," which may protect against cancer.

Variations   Use ½ cauliflower with a large peeled celeriac, or try ¾-pound peeled Jerusalem artichokes steamed with cauliflower. Add a dash of truffle oil or any herb-flavored olive oil or use horseradish sauce.

☠ kid friendly without horseradish cream.

PUMPKIN AND GINGER MASH

SERVES 4

prep time: 5 minutes

cook time: 15 minutes

2	cups pumpkin chopped (about 10 ounces)
½	ripe head cauliflower chopped (about 12–14 ounces)
¼	cup chicken stock
2	teaspoons freshly grated ginger (optional)
1	tablespoon butter
	sea salt

Microwave pumpkin and cauliflower in chicken stock or steam until soft, about 10–15 minutes. Drain, retaining stock. Add ginger and butter and process or blend, adding a little more stock if required. Serve as a bed for beef, lamb or chicken.

Note   If you're watching every carb, this mash and variation should be avoided – use cauliflower mash until you reach your ideal size. Ginger may not work with all the components of the meal, so if in doubt, leave out.

Variation   Use sweet potato instead of pumpkin, although sweet potato is slightly higher in carbs. Roast pumpkin or sweet potato in its skin instead of steaming, for a delicious difference.

🦂 *kid friendly* without ginger.

Opposite: Herb-Salted Turnip and Sweet Potato Chips (page 151)

BROCCOLI AND PARSNIP MASH

SERVES 4

prep time: 5 minutes

cook time: 15 minutes

½   **head broccoli (about 10 ounces), roughly chopped**

1   **large parsnip (about 8 ounces), peeled and roughly chopped**

2   **carrots (about 8 ounces), peeled and roughly chopped**

¼   **cup chicken or vegetable stock**

1   **tablespoon butter**

    sea salt

Microwave all vegetables in stock or steam until very soft, about 10–15 minutes. Strain, reserving liquid if microwaved. Add butter and salt to taste. Blend or process, adding more stock if needed.

Note   See picture of this dish opposite page 171.

Variation   Parsnips are not a low-carb vegetable so replace with ¼ ripe head of cauliflower (about 8 ounces) to reduce your carbs.

🌸 *kid friendly* with grated mozzarella on top.

Opposite: Tandoori Chicken with Cucumber Salad (page 92)

BABY BEETS AND GREEN BEANS WITH GOAT CHEESE

SERVES 4

prep time: 5 minutes

cook time: 10 minutes

1	bunch baby beets (about 10 ounces) or 2 beets
	olive oil/olive oil spray
1	large red onion, cut into wedges, retaining base
4	handfuls green beans (about 8 ounces), tops trimmed
¼	cup goat cheese marinated in oil (about 2 ounces)
	sea salt
	cracked pepper

Trim stalks of beets leaving about $^3/_4$-inch. Steam or microwave until just cooked, about 5 minutes. Remove and slice baby beets into halves or quarters depending on their size (slice larger beets into 8 wedges). Heat a large non-stick frying pan or wok over medium to high heat. When hot, spray or brush well with oil and add onion. Cook for 1–2 minutes and then add beans to pan. Cook for a minute longer, then add beets, tossing well. Place vegetables in a bowl, crumble cheese and drizzle a little olive oil from cheese over the top. Season with salt and pepper. Serve either warm or cold with beef, lamb, chicken, pork or turkey.

Note   Steam or microwave beans for 2–3 minutes if you prefer less crunch. If using normal-sized beets, cut into quarters before steaming, still retaining stalks.

Variations   Add a handful of chopped cilantro. Replace green beans with 7 ounces baby turnips, cooked and prepared the same way as beets. Add a cup of roasted sweet potato or pumpkin cut into $^3/_4$-inch cubes for a higher- carb but delicious alternative. Use feta, ricotta or plain yogurt for a lower-fat alternative to goat cheese.

BROCCOLI, OLIVES AND FETA

SERVES 4

prep time: 5 minutes

cook time: 5 minutes

12	**kalamata olives**
1	**pound broccoli**
1	**tablespoon olive oil**
4	**tablespoons low-fat feta marinated in oil**
	sea salt
	cracked pepper

Slice olives in half horizontally. Cut broccoli into large bite-sized pieces and steam for 2–3 minutes. Heat a saucepan over medium heat. When hot, add oil, olives and broccoli and gently toss. Remove from heat and crumble feta over broccoli and season with salt and pepper. Serve on the side with lamb, chicken, beef or veal.

Note   Broccoli, a cruciferous vegetable, is an excellent source of vitamin C, a good source of beta carotene, contains iron, potassium and folate and may even prevent cancer! Do not boil broccoli as you will lose half of its vitamin C content.

Variation   Use broccolini instead of broccoli.

SAUCES, SALSAS and MARINADES

Intense flavors and variety are the key to successfully maintaining a low-carb lifestyle.

A piece of grilled chicken with a tomato and lettuce salad can sustain your interest for only so long. But with a little extra effort, a main meal can be transformed. Marinate chicken in parsley, lemon and verjuice or serve with a spicy roasted red pepper sauce. Drizzle a simple green salad with a Thai lime or Chinese soy dressing, dollop some creamy avocado mash, watermelon and cucumber salsa or mint and cilantro chutney on your plate to accompany anything from simple barbecued lamb and grilled fish to lemongrass and ginger chicken balls. Basil pesto and roasted tomato sauce are invaluable and flexible condiments. The tomato sauce forms an integral part of many soups and main courses, including both slow-baking dishes and instant tasty meals.

Use this chapter together with chapter 5, Meaty Mains, as the foundation for endless combinations of delicious and variety-packed meals. The chutneys and sauces are delicious and most keep for up to a week. They also add interesting flavors to a quick snack – spread a little light cream cheese and roasted red pepper sauce over a baked eggplant slice and roll it up; spread dill and mustard sauce over a piece of smoked salmon or trout; dollop tomato and red pepper relish over low-fat shredded ham or shaved turkey and wrap it up in an iceberg or romaine lettuce leaf. Unleash your imagination.

ROASTED TOMATO SAUCE

prep time: 5 minutes

cook time: 45 minutes

1	**large red onion, thickly sliced**
6	**cloves garlic**
10	**ripe tomatoes (about 2½ pounds), halved**
1	**tablespoon olive oil**
1	**teaspoon sea salt**
1	**tablespoon balsamic vinegar**

-Preheat oven to 400°F. Place onion and garlic on a large non-stick baking tray or tray lined with parchment paper and arrange tomato cut-side down on top. Drizzle with oil and sprinkle with salt, and bake for 45 minutes or until tomato is soft and onion is cooked. Allow to cool, then squeeze garlic out of skins (each clove should pop out easily). Place tomato mixture in a bowl and add balsamic vinegar. Blend or process until smooth.

Serve with pizza, soup, vegetables – anything goes!

Note   The sauce keeps for up to 2 weeks refrigerated in an airtight container and freezes well too.

Variation   Canned tomatoes work well here. For this recipe, use 3 cans peeled tomatoes (no added sugar).

🐝 *kid friendly*

ROASTED RED PEPPER SAUCE

MAKES 1 $^1/_2$ CUPS

prep time: 5 minutes

cook time: 30 minutes

3	**red peppers**
1	**teaspoon olive oil**
1	**red onion, chopped**
2	**anchovy fillets**
½	**cup chicken stock**

Preheat oven to 425°F or turn grill on high. Cut peppers in half lengthwise. Remove pith and seeds. Place cut-side down on a non-stick baking tray or tray lined with parchment paper. Bake or grill for 20 minutes or until skin darkens and blisters. Heat olive oil in a saucepan over medium heat. Add onion and cook for 2–3 minutes or until soft. Remove peppers and place in a plastic bag for 10 minutes, then peel and roughly chop. Add anchovy, chicken stock and peppers to saucepan and bring to the boil. Reduce heat and simmer, covered, for 5–10 minutes. Blend or purée until smooth. Serve with chicken, lamb, turkey, frittatas and omelets.

Note   Grilled or roasted peppers will keep for up to 7 days refrigerated in an airtight glass jar. Peppers are an excellent source of vitamin C, with red peppers containing 3 times more vitamin C than green. Bottled or canned red peppers provide a quick alternative to grilling or roasting, although the flavor is not as sweet or intense.

BASIL PESTO

MAKES 1 ¹/₄ CUPS

prep time: 10 minutes

cook time: 10 minutes

¾	**cup pine nuts**
2	**handfuls basil**
2	**cloves garlic**
1½	**cups grated Parmesan**
½	**cup olive oil**
1	**teaspoon sea salt**
	cracked pepper

Preheat oven to 400°F. Dry roast pine nuts for 10 minutes or until golden brown. Process or blend basil, garlic, roasted pine nuts and Parmesan until finely chopped. Add oil gradually and pulse until mixture is smooth.

Serve with soups; spread over mushrooms and sliced tomatoes and bake; toss a tablespoon with steamed asparagus; spread a little over turkey, lamb or chicken before cooking; add a little to omelets and frittatas; and toss with cooked tofu served on roasted tomato sauce with shaved Parmesan.

Note   To store, press plastic wrap over contents or place thin layer of olive oil on top to prevent browning. Store in a screw-top jar and refrigerate. It will keep for up to 2 weeks.

Variation   Replace basil with cilantro or mint and/or use walnuts or cashews instead of pine nuts.

🐞 *kid friendly*

CUCUMBER AND MINT YOGURT SAUCE

MAKES ABOUT 1 CUP

prep time: 5 minutes

½ cup low-fat plain yogurt
1 English cucumber, finely chopped
3 tablespoons freshly chopped mint
1 clove garlic, finely chopped
1 tablespoon lemon juice
  sea salt

Gently combine all ingredients in a bowl and mix well. Serve with grilled chicken and lamb cutlets, tandoori lamb or chicken. This sauce teams well with mint and cilantro chutney (see page 170).

🌸 *kid friendly*

DILL AND MUSTARD SAUCE

MAKES ¹/₂ CUP

prep time: 2 minutes

1 tablespoon Dijon mustard
4 tablespoons flaxseed oil or extra virgin olive oil
4 tablespoons lemon juice
2 tablespoons freshly chopped dill
  pinch of sea salt

Place all ingredients in an airtight glass jar and shake vigorously. Serve with ham, smoked salmon, mackerel or trout.

PICKLED GINGER AND SOY DIPPING SAUCE

MAKES ABOUT $^1/_3$ CUP

prep time: 2 minutes

4	**tablespoons light soy**
2	**tablespoons rice vinegar**
2	**teaspoons pickled ginger, finely sliced**

Place all ingredients in a jar and shake well. Serve with chicken balls, Thai fish cakes or Japanese salmon sushi rolls (see chapter 2).

Variation   Add a very finely sliced green onion or $^1/_2$ small seeded chile pepper for extra bite.

THAI LIME DRESSING

MAKES $^2/_3$ CUP

prep time: 5 minutes

4	**tablespoons fresh lime juice**
2	**tablespoons light soy**
2	**tablespoons sesame oil**
2	**tablespoons fish sauce**
½	**small red chile, seeded and finely chopped**
2	**tablespoons freshly chopped cilantro**
2	**tablespoons freshly chopped mint**

Place all ingredients in a jar and shake vigorously.

Note   For extra zing use Vietnamese mint, which is available at some markets and Asian grocers. If you're making this dressing the day before or in the morning, do not add herbs until just prior to serving. If you have dressing left over, remove herbs by straining and add more fresh herbs prior to serving the next time.

Variation   Add a stalk of finely sliced lemongrass. Use lemon juice if lime is not available.

CHINESE SOY AND SESAME DRESSING

MAKES $^1/_2$ CUP

prep time: 5 minutes

4	**tablespoons light soy**
2	**tablespoons sesame oil**
2	**cloves garlic, crushed**
6	**tablespoons rice wine vinegar**
2	**tablespoons lemon juice**
2	**tablespoons freshly grated ginger**

Place all ingredients in a jar and shake vigorously. Use to dress coleslaws or simple green salads. It's good with chicken slaw and Chinese cabbage, red pepper, shredded beets and cashews.

Note   This dressing keeps for up to 1 week refrigerated in an airtight glass jar.

Variation   Use 1 tablespoon shredded pickled ginger instead of fresh ginger. For a bit of spice add a fresh chile pepper or 2 star anise, a Chinese spice available from specialized Asian groceries and some supermarkets.

LEMON CAESAR DRESSING

MAKES $^2/_3$ CUP

prep time: 5 minutes

4	**tablespoons white wine vinegar**
1	**teaspoon Dijon mustard**
1	**egg**
1	**clove garlic, crushed**
2	**anchovy fillets, finely chopped**
1	**tablespoon lemon juice**
½	**cup extra virgin olive oil**
	sea salt
	cracked pepper

Combine all ingredients except oil in a bowl or processor until smooth. Add oil gradually. Season with salt and pepper to taste. Serve with a simple green salad, chicken Caesar and arugula, pear and pan-toasted walnuts (see page 133).

Note   This dressing keeps for 3–4 days refrigerated in an airtight jar.

kid friendly

BALSAMIC AND GARLIC DRESSING

MAKES 1 CUP

prep time: 2 minutes

⅓ **cup balsamic vinegar**
⅔ **cup virgin olive oil**
1 **teaspoon Dijon mustard**
6 **cloves garlic**
½ **teaspoon sea salt**

Place all ingredients in a jar and shake vigorously. Drizzle over a simple green salad or roasted vegetables (see page 147), leaving cloves to infuse remaining dressing.

Note   This dressing keeps for up to 2 weeks refrigerated in an airtight glass jar.

Variation   Use malt vinegar instead of balsamic.

YOGURT AND LIME DRESSING

SERVES 4

prep time: 5 minutes

3 **tablespoons low-fat plain yogurt**
1 **tablespoon lime juice**
2 **teaspoons freshly grated ginger**
3 **tablespoons freshly chopped mint (optional)**

Combine all ingredients and mix well. Serve with fish, grilled chicken or cucumber salad (see chapter 6).

HORSERADISH CREAM

SERVES 4

prep time: 5 minutes

6	tablespoons light sour cream
2	tablespoons freshly grated horseradish
2	tablespoons white wine vinegar
2	teaspoons Dijon mustard
½	teaspoon salt

Place contents in a small mixing bowl and whisk vigorously. Serve with beef, smoked salmon or trout.

Note   This keeps for up to 7 days refrigerated in an airtight glass jar. Use bottled horseradish when fresh horseradish is not in season.

RED PEPPER MAYONNAISE

MAKES ABOUT $^1/_2$ CUP

prep time: 2 minutes

cook time: 20 minutes

2	red peppers
2	tablespoons low-fat mayonnaise
2	tablespoons low-fat plain yogurt
1	clove garlic
½	fresh chile pepper, seeded

Preheat oven to 425°F or turn grill to high. Cut peppers in half lengthwise and remove pith and seeds. Place cut-side down on a non-stick baking tray or tray lined with parchment paper and bake or grill for 20 minutes, or until pepper blisters and blackens. Remove from oven and place in a plastic bag for 10 minutes, then peel. Place all ingredients in a processor and blend together to form a smooth sauce. Serve with lamb, beef, chicken, turkey or veal.

Note   Bottled or canned red peppers make a good, quick alternative to roasting or grilling your own. This keeps for 2 to 3 days in an airtight glass jar, refrigerated.

🌼 *kid friendly* without the chile pepper.

BASIL MAYONNAISE

SERVES 4

prep time: 2 minutes

2	**tablespoons low-fat plain yogurt**
2	**tablespoons low-fat mayonnaise**
1	**tablespoon freshly chopped basil**
2	**teaspoons *basil pesto*** **(see page 162)**

Combine ingredients in a bowl and mix well. Serve with lamb, beef, chicken, turkey or veal.

Note   This mayonnaise keeps for 2 to 3 days refrigerated in airtight glass jar.

Variation   Replace fresh basil and pesto with fresh cilantro and cilantro pesto (see this chapter).

SPICY RED PEPPER CHUTNEY

MAKES 1 CUP

prep time: 10 minutes

cook time: 20 minutes

4	**red peppers**
2	**cloves garlic**
½	**cup walnuts**
½	**teaspoon cumin**
¼	**teaspoon cayenne pepper** **pinch of sea salt**

Preheat oven to 425°F or turn grill to high. Cut peppers in half lengthwise and remove pith and seeds. Place cut-side down on a non-stick baking tray or tray lined with parchment paper and bake or grill for 20 minutes, or until pepper blisters and blackens. Remove from oven and place in plastic bag for 10 minutes, then peel. Add to processor with remaining ingredients and blend to form a thick paste. Serve with lamb, beef or chicken.

Note   This chutney will keep for several days in a tightly sealed jar, refrigerated.

Variation   For additional spice and fiber, add ½ chile pepper.

MINT AND CILANTRO CHUTNEY

MAKES 1 CUP

prep time: 5 minutes

1	**handful cilantro**
3	**handfuls mint**
½	**red onion**
1	**teaspoon sea salt**
2	**cloves garlic**
¼	**cup lime juice**
1	**tablespoon fish sauce**
½	**teaspoon sambal oelek (chile paste)**

Finely chop all ingredients and mix well or blend in a food processor until well combined. Serve with grilled or barbecued lamb, chicken or fish.

Note This chutney will keep for 2 days in an airtight glass jar, refrigerated, but it is best eaten on the day because it does lose some color and flavor over time. This chutney is delicious teamed with tzatziki or cucumber and mint yogurt sauce (see page 163).

AVOCADO AND TOMATO SALSA

SERVES 4

prep time: 5 minutes

1	**avocado, finely chopped**
2	**ripe tomatoes, seeded and finely cubed**
¼	**red onion, finely cubed**
2	**tablespoons freshly chopped cilantro**
2	**teaspoons raspberry vinegar or lemon juice**
	sea salt
	cracked pepper

Gently combine all ingredients in a medium-sized bowl. Season with salt and pepper to taste. Serve with fish or chicken.

Note Salsas make a good accompaniment for any dish and work well as a side salad.

Variations Use ½ mango or peach in addition to, or instead of, avocado. Cut into long, thin slices. Replace cilantro with mint. Serve as a side salad and add 1 tablespoon baby capers for extra bite.

Opposite: Lamb, Eggplant and Feta with Roasted Red Pepper Sauce (page 119)

MANGO AND AVOCADO SALSA

SERVES 4

prep time: 5 minutes

½   **avocado, finely cubed**
½   **mango, finely cubed**
1   **English cucumber, finely cubed**
2   **tablespoons freshly chopped mint**
1   **tablespoon fish sauce**
1   **teaspoon lemon juice**

Gently combine all ingredients in a medium-sized bowl until well mixed. Serve with fish or chicken.

Variations   Use cilantro instead of mint. Replace mango with 1 tomato for a lower-carb alternative. Chop ingredients into chunky cubes or long slices, add red onion and serve as a side salad. For more flavor add ¼ red onion and ½ roasted or chargrilled red pepper.

WATERMELON AND CUCUMBER SALSA

SERVES 4

prep time: 5 minutes

1   **cup watermelon, seeded, cubed**
1   **English cucumber, peeled and cubed**
2   **tablespoons freshly chopped cilantro (optional)**
1   **tablespoon lime juice**

Gently mix watermelon, cucumber and cilantro together, then squeeze over lime juice. Serve with fish, chicken or turkey.

Variations   For a slightly different flavor, substitute lemon juice for lime juice and parsley for cilantro. Use 1 cup pineapple instead of watermelon and add ¼ red onion and a small seeded red chile pepper for a little kick. These variations are delicious with grilled pork or veal cutlets marinated in spicy Asian marinade.

🐾 *kid friendly* without cilantro.

Opposite: Beef and Mushrooms in Red Wine (page 103) with Broccoli and Parsnip Mash (page 155)

CILANTRO, PARSLEY AND LEMON SALSA

SERVES 4

prep time: 5 minutes

1	**small handful cilantro**
1	**small handful flat-leaf parsley**
2	**tablespoons lemon juice**
2	**tablespoons lemon rind**
2	**cloves garlic**

Roughly blend all ingredients until just combined. Serve with veal or lamb shank, Moroccan lamb soup or Moroccan chicken (see chapters 3 and 5).

Variations   Omit cilantro and double parsley or substitute fresh basil or rosemary for cilantro, depending on the flavors of the dish this is accompanying. Add 1 tablespoon olive oil and use as a marinade for fish or chicken.

CAPERS, BASIL AND MINT SALSA

MAKES 1 CUP

prep time: 5 minutes

1	**handful flat-leaf parsley**
1	**handful mint**
1	**handful basil**
2	**cloves garlic**
2	**tablespoons capers**
1	**tablespoon olive oil**
2	**tablespoons lemon juice**
	pinch of sea salt

Blend or process all ingredients until combined but still chunky. Serve with lamb, veal, fish or chicken.

Note   This salsa keeps for 3 to 4 days refrigerated in an airtight glass jar, but it's best used on the day as the color diminishes thereafter. Like the cilantro, parsley and lemon salsa above, this is more a herb chutney or chermoula than a salsa.

Variation   Add 6 kalamata olives or 6 anchovy fillets.

TOMATO AND RED PEPPER RELISH

MAKES 1 CUP

prep time: 5 minutes

2   vine-ripened tomatoes
2   red peppers, seeded
1   fresh chile pepper (optional), seeded
2   cloves garlic
½   red onion
2   tablespoons balsamic vinegar
2   handfuls cilantro
2   tablespoons lemon juice

Blend or process all ingredients, until smooth. Serve with frittata or chicken or add a tablespoon to an omelet or scrambled eggs. Pour into shot glasses and serve chilled with pre-dinner drinks.

Note   For extra kick do not seed the chile pepper. Relish will keep refrigerated for up to 1 week in an airtight glass jar.

Variation   Try red wine vinegar instead of balsamic and use basil instead of cilantro.

AVOCADO MASH

SERVES 4

prep time: 5 minutes

1   ripe avocado, mashed
¼   red onion, finely chopped
1   teaspoon white wine vinegar
1–2   tablespoons lime or lemon juice
       sea salt
       cracked pepper

Combine all ingredients and season with salt and pepper to taste. Serve with chicken, turkey, lamb, beef or fish or as a dip.

Note   Make this mash just prior to serving so that it retains its fresh green color. Another great side dish or condiment to use for barbecues or when entertaining large numbers.

Variations   Add ½ finely chopped red pepper or seeded tomato, chopped cilantro or mint, or ½ chopped chile pepper.

LIME, GARLIC AND SOY MARINADE

SERVES 4

prep time: 5 minutes

2	**limes**
4	**cloves garlic, crushed**
2	**teaspoons grated ginger**
4	**tablespoons light soy**

Cut limes into quarters and squeeze 3 tablespoons lime juice into bowl. Add lime skins, garlic, ginger and soy and mix well. Marinate chicken, pork and fish.

Note   Use lemons if limes are unavailable.

Variations   Add 2 lemongrass stalks, chopped and crushed, and $1/2$ finely chopped chile pepper or $1/2$ teaspoon crushed red pepper flakes. Try adding $1/2$ teaspoon Chinese five spice, 1 teaspoon star anise and 2 tablespoons teriyaki for a deeper Asian flavor.

☠ *kid friendly* using lemon without the variations.

CHILE AND SOYBEAN MARINADE

SERVES 4

prep time: 5 minutes

1	**tablespoon sesame oil**
2	**tablespoons red wine vinegar**
4	**tablespoons light soy**
1	**tablespoon chile paste with fermented soybean**
2	**tablespoons water**
1	**tablespoon tomato paste**

Combine all ingredients in a bowl and mix well. Marinate veal, chicken, pork or turkey.

Variation   Use rice wine vinegar instead of red wine vinegar for a sweeter option.

SWEET PEANUT MARINADE

SERVES 4

prep time: 5 minutes

1 **tablespoon light soy**
1 **tablespoon peanut butter**
1 **tablespoon pure maple syrup**
1 **teaspoon tomato paste**
1 **teaspoon sesame oil**
1 **tablespoon lemon juice**

Combine all ingredients in a bowl or glass jar and mix well. Marinate chicken, veal or pork by lightly spreading over both sides of meat. Spread remaining marinade over the top of meat once cooked.

Note   Maple syrup makes this marinade higher in carbohydrates than some other marinades, but it is natural and delicious with some nutritional value.

🌸 *kid friendly*

MUSTARD, LEMON AND VERJUICE

MAKES 1 CUP

prep time: 5 minutes

1 **handful finely chopped parsley**
2 **tablespoons lemon zest**
2 **tablespoons lemon juice**
2 **tablespoons verjuice**
1 **tablespoon olive oil**
2 **tablespoons Dijon mustard**
1 **clove garlic**

Blend all ingredients in a bowl or glass jar. Marinate chicken, pork or fish.

Variation   Substitute 4 tablespoons fresh tarragon or dill for parsley.

Note   Verjuice is made from pressed, unripened white grapes. It is slightly acidic and used in cooking.

🌸 *kid friendly* without lemon juice.

HERB SALT

MAKES 7 TABLESPOONS

prep time: 5 minutes

3	**tablespoons dried rosemary**
1	**teaspoon dried oregano**
1	**teaspoon onion powder**
3	**tablespoons sea salt**
3	**bay leaves, finely crushed**

Mix all ingredients together. Store in an airtight jar. Sprinkle over vegetable chips, chicken, turkey, beef, lamb, pork, veal or fish prior to grilling, barbecuing or baking.

CAJUN SPICES

MAKES 5 TABLESPOONS

prep time: 5 minutes

1	**tablespoon onion powder**
2	**teaspoons garlic powder**
2	**teaspoons cracked pepper**
2	**teaspoons cayenne**
1	**tablespoon sweet paprika**
1	**tablespoon oregano**

Combine all spices and store in an airtight glass jar. Sprinkle over fish, chicken, beef, lamb or pork and chargrill or barbecue.

MOROCCAN SPICE RUB

MAKES 5 TABLESPOONS

prep time: 5 minutes

1	**tablespoon powdered ginger**
1	**tablespoon cumin**
1	**tablespoon sweet paprika**
1	**tablespoon turmeric**
1	**teaspoon cinnamon**

Combine all spices and store in an airtight glass jar. Sprinkle over fish, chicken, beef, lamb or pork and chargrill or barbecue.

MAKES 7 QUARTS

prep time: 5 minutes

cook time: 2 hours

1	**whole chicken**
1	**chicken carcass**
2	**carrots, roughly chopped**
3	**stalks celery and leaves, roughly chopped**
2	**yellow onions, roughly chopped**
1	**sprig thyme**
1	**handful freshly chopped parsley**
3	**bay leaves**
12	**whole peppercorns**
2	**gallons cold water**
1	**teaspoon sea salt**

Place all ingredients in a large saucepan and bring to the boil. Reduce heat and simmer, covered, for 1 hour or until whole chicken is cooked. Remove surface scum as it appears. Remove whole chicken and set aside. Simmer, uncovered, for a further hour, removing any sediment/scum that forms. Strain stock into a large bowl, discarding vegetables. Allow stock to cool and then remove fat from the surface.

Note   Remove skin from the whole chicken and use meat for salads, snacks or casseroles. Combine leftover chicken meat with a couple of handfuls of spinach and roasted vegetables, then sprinkle with crumbled feta for a delicious low-carbohydrate salad. If you have the time, allow stock to cool before straining as this strengthens the flavor. Freeze excess stock in 2-cup quantities.

Variations   My neighbor Mandy is the queen of chicken stock and uses 2 chicken leg-thigh sections and a turkey wing or drumstick instead of the carcass and herbs for a very smooth and full-bodied stock. For a good vegetable stock follow this recipe but omit chicken and carcass. Add 2 parsnips, 2 leeks, 2 tomatoes and 1 cup mushrooms. Roughly chop all vegetables. Add 8 cloves peeled garlic. By grilling or baking lightly oiled vegetables and adding a variety of fresh herbs you will considerably change the flavor of the stock.

🥀 *kid friendly*   To 6 cups simmering stock, add some cooked shredded chicken, corn, sliced broccoli and thin egg noodles. Drizzle in 2 beaten eggs and you have a complete meal.

DESSERTS
and AFTER...

-I am usually satisfied after my main meal and rarely desire another course – but when I do

feel like something sweet, I have a few favorites, such as the baked peach with macadamia nut

crumble or, for something instant, the strawberry, coconut and macaroon tarts. My dislike for

"low-carb/no-carb" manufactured artificial sugars, such as Sucralose, Nutrasweet and aspartame,

means that some of the dishes are verging on "tart" rather than sweet. Using jam, maple syrup

and apple juice concentrate will bump up the carbs – but if you're eating dessert, so be it.

If you want to avoid these additional carbs you may wish to experiment with an approved,

low-carb artificial sweetener. Splenda, which is actually made from sugar, is probably the pick of

the crop and at 1.9 calories per teaspoon with no fat and no carb, as compared to 16 calories per

teaspoon of sugar, it will appeal to many dessert junkies. If you are sticking to the low-glycemic index foods then you may wish to use fructose, a natural "simple" sugar that is

derived from fruit and is available from health food stores. Fructose is also sweeter than ordinary

sugar so you don't have to use as much. In my low-fat days, I rarely considered eating dessert

but would always devour several low-fat raisin cookies, which were loaded with sugar. I now

focus on the low-carb fruits – berries, melons, peaches, plums, kiwifruit and pears – for

something sweet and to make the most of their nutritional advantages and fiber. Just

occasionally I also indulge in a little dark chocolate (with 70 percent cocoa).

For many people, these desserts will come nowhere near their usual requirement of

"sweetness." After several weeks of restricting your sugar intake, however, you will be

surprised at how quickly your sweet tooth subsides.

BAKED PEAR WITH ALMOND AND COCONUT CRUMBLE

SERVES 4

prep time: 5 minutes

cook time: 40 minutes

4	**tablespoons shredded coconut**
4	**tablespoons almond meal**
2	**teaspoons grated ginger (optional)**
2	**ripe small–medium pears, halved and cored**
1	**egg, lightly beaten**
	macadamia nut oil/spray
	pure cream

Preheat oven to 425°F. Combine coconut, almond meal and ginger. Dip pear into egg, then press the cut-side of pear into coconut mixture. Place on a tray lined with parchment paper and sprinkle remaining crumble mixture over pear. Spray or brush well with oil. Bake for 30–40 minutes or until pear is golden and cooked through. Serve with a drizzle of cream.

Note   If crumble browns too quickly, cover with foil and remove foil 5 minutes prior to taking dish out of the oven. See picture of this dish opposite page 187.

BAKED PEACH WITH BLACKBERRY JAM AND MACADAMIA NUT

SERVES 4

prep time: 5 minutes

cook time: 30 minutes

2   **ripe peaches, halved and pitted**
2   **teaspoons blackberry jam (no added sugar)**
2   **tablespoons shredded or shaved coconut (unsweetened)**
1   **teaspoon orange zest**
2   **tablespoons macadamia nuts, lightly crushed**
    macadamia nut oil/spray
    pure cream

Preheat oven to 400°F. Spread a layer of jam over each peach half and sprinkle with coconut, orange zest and macadamia nuts. Place on a tray lined with parchment paper and lightly spray or brush with oil. Bake for 30 minutes. Serve with a drizzle of cream.

Note   If peaches are unavailable use canned peaches in natural juices.

Variations   Try fresh ricotta sprinkled with mint, nutmeg or cinnamon for a lower-fat option. Use 4 nectarines instead of peaches. This recipe is also delicious as a side dish, without the cream, of course, served with a piece of grilled chicken and salad.

STEWED PLUMS WITH BERRY YOGURT AND BITTERSWEET CHOCOLATE

SERVES 2

prep time: 5 minutes

cook time: 10 minutes

1	vanilla bean
½	cup water
1	tablespoon apple juice concentrate
1	teaspoon rosewater essence (optional)
6	plums, halved and pitted
4	tablespoons whole-milk berry yogurt
1	tablespoon shaved dark chocolate

Slice vanilla bean in half lengthwise. Place water, vanilla bean, apple juice concentrate and rosewater essence in a saucepan and bring to the boil. Reduce heat, add plums and simmer, covered, for 10 minutes.

To serve, spoon plums into a shallow bowl and dollop with yogurt and sprinkle with chocolate.

Note The plums are excellent for breakfast with a dollop of ricotta or yogurt. Or spoon a little over your porridge. Chocolate is high in fat, but good-quality dark, bitter chocolate is made of 70-percent cocoa and has the least sugar of any chocolate. It's actually very good for you as it contains endorphins, which make you feel great, as well as iron and anti-cancer and anti-heart disease chemicals.

Variations Use ricotta instead of yogurt or simply drizzle with a little pure cream. Any combination of peaches, pears, apples, apricots, plums and berries can be used with similar success. The cooking time will vary depending on the fruit used; just keep checking. If you're using berries, cook the other fruit first then remove from heat and add berries at the last minute.

POACHED PEARS IN RED WINE AND CINNAMON

SERVES 2

prep time: 2 minutes

cook time: 20 minutes

1	**tablespoon lemon zest**
1	**cinnamon stick**
1	**tablespoon apple juice concentrate**
½	**cup water**
¾	**cup red wine**
2	**Bosc pears**
4	**tablespoons whole-milk berry yogurt**

Place lemon zest in a medium saucepan with crumbled cinnamon stick, apple juice concentrate, water and red wine. Simmer over low heat, covered, for 5 minutes. Meanwhile, peel pears and cut vertically into quarters removing core and seeds. Add pears and simmer for 10–15 minutes or until just cooked, turning pears regularly and basting with syrup.

To serve, place 4 pear segments in a bowl, dollop with yogurt and drizzle with a little wine syrup.

Note   Cooking time will vary depending on the firmness of the pears.

Variation   Use water instead of wine for a breakfast option.

🌸 *kid friendly* with water instead of wine.

BAKED APPLE IN BRANDY WITH CINNAMON RICOTTA

SERVES 4

prep time: 5 minutes

cook time: 40 minutes

4	small red apples (small enough to fit into small ramekins), covered
1	tablespoon butter
1	tablespoon brandy
1	tablespoon maple syrup
2	tablespoons pistachios
½	cup low-fat smooth ricotta
1	teaspoon cinnamon
4	cinnamon sticks

Preheat oven to 425°F. Place each apple into individual ramekins. Melt butter in microwave and mix with brandy and maple syrup. Drizzle 1 tablespoon butter mixture over each apple and bake for 40 minutes. Meanwhile, place pistachios on a non-stick baking tray or tray lined with parchment paper and bake for 5–7 minutes or until golden brown. Mix cinnamon and ricotta.

To serve, turn out ramekin and place apple and syrup on a plate. Dollop with cinnamon ricotta and place a cinnamon stick in each apple.

Note   Cooking time for different apples varies. They are ready when soft to touch.

Variation   Use Grand Marnier or any similar liqueur instead of brandy.

BERRY AND PEACH TART

prep time: 5 minutes

cook time: 45 minutes

	olive oil/olive oil spray
½	cup mixed berries
2	peaches, sliced
2	nectarines, sliced
1	tablespoon blackberry jam (no added sugar)
1	teaspoon maple syrup or apple juice concentrate
1	piece soft flat bread
	macadamia nut oil/spray
2	tablespoons shredded or shaved coconut
	pure cream

Preheat oven to 350°F. Lightly spray a non-stick 8-inch cake pan with olive oil. Arrange fruit in layers in pan. Spoon jam into a small saucepan and heat gently until it melts. Brush over fruit, then drizzle over maple syrup. Bake for 20 minutes. Meanwhile cut flat bread into a 8-inch round. Spray or brush with macadamia nut oil and place over cooked fruit. Return to oven for 15 minutes or until bread is crisp. Meanwhile place coconut on a tray lined with parchment paper and dry roast until golden. When tart is cooked, turn out onto a dish at once.

To serve, cut tart into wedges, place on plates, sprinkle with coconut and drizzle with a little cream.

Note   When fresh berries and stone fruits are unavailable, use 1 large green apple, a large pear, both peeled, and 1 cup frozen berries or canned peaches or apricots, using similar quantities to those in recipe.

Variations   Use apricots instead of nectarines. Sprinkle with roasted flaked almonds instead of coconut. Reduce the carbohydrate content by leaving out the flat bread and simply baking the fruit. Add 1 teaspoon grated ginger to melted jam and syrup, drizzle over fruit and bake for 35 minutes. Then sprinkle with coconut and raw nuts such as slivered almonds or crushed hazelnuts.

CANTALOUPE AND BERRIES WITH WARM RASPBERRY SAUCE

prep time: 5 minutes

cook time: 5 minutes

1½	cups raspberries
½	cup blueberries
1	teaspoon mixed fruits jam (no added sugar)
1	teaspoon vanilla extract
2	tablespoons water
½	cantaloupe, peeled and cut into wedges
1	tablespoon finely chopped mint (optional)
4	scoops low-fat vanilla ice cream

Combine 1 cup raspberries, jam, vanilla and water in a medium saucepan and bring to the boil. Reduce heat and simmer for 2–3 minutes. Then blend or purée to make a smooth sauce.

To serve, arrange canteloupe and scatter remaining berries over the top. Drizzle with warm sauce, sprinkle with mint and serve with a small scoop of ice cream.

Note   See picture of this opposite.

Variations   Use passionfruit, strawberries, blackberries or any combination. Substitute low-fat berry yogurt for ice cream for a lower-fat alternative.

PINEAPPLE WITH SILKEN TOFU, CINNAMON SYRUP AND COCONUT CREAM

SERVES 4

prep time: 5 minutes

cook time: 5 minutes

1	cinnamon stick
½	cup water
1	tablespoon apple juice concentrate
4	ounces silken tofu
4	whole slices pineapple (about ⅓-inch thick), roughly chopped
2	tablespoons light coconut cream
2	tablespoons crushed hazelnuts

Break cinnamon stick in half. Place water, apple juice and cinnamon stick in a large saucepan and bring to the boil, covered. Remove from heat. Carefully cut tofu block into 4 equal slices. Gently place tofu in apple juice syrup and bring to the boil. Reduce heat and simmer for 1–2 minutes.

To serve, place each slice of tofu in a bowl. Stack pineapple on top and drizzle with syrup and a little coconut cream. Sprinkle with hazelnuts.

Opposite: Baked Pear with Almond and Coconut Crumble (page 180)

STRAWBERRY, COCONUT AND MACAROON TARTS

MAKES 8 TARTS

prep time: 2 minutes

8	**coconut macaroons**
4	**teaspoons light cream and cottage cheese blend**
8	**strawberries, quartered**

Spread ½-teaspoon cheese blend over each macaroon and place strawberry segments on top.

Note   This is more a companion for tea or coffee than dessert.

Variations   Use sliced fresh figs, raspberries or blueberries instead of strawberries. Try mini crispbreads instead of macaroons for only 1 carb each. Make a berry sandwich by adding a little maple syrup to cream cheese and placing another crispbread on top. Add finely chopped kiwifruit, passionfruit or a little sugar-free jam or lemon rind and juice to cream cheese for a change in color, texture and taste.

kid friendly

BLACKBERRY AND MASCARPONE CIGARS

prep time: 5 minutes

cook time: 15 minutes

1	tablespoon lemon zest
2	teaspoons lemon juice
1	tablespoon mascarpone or light cream and cottage cheese blend or ricotta
1	teaspoon blackberry jam (no added sugar)
1	tablespoon shredded coconut
1	piece barley soft flat bread
	macadamia nut oil/spray
1	cup blackberries, blueberries, raspberries or strawberries
	pure cream
2	teaspoons maple syrup

Preheat oven to 400°F. Mix together lemon zest, juice, mascarpone, jam and 2 teaspoons coconut to form a paste. Cut bread in half diagonally to make 2 triangles. Spread paste evenly over each triangle and roll into 2 thin cigars. Sprinkle remaining coconut over the top and spray with oil. Bake for 10–15 minutes or until coconut is golden.

To serve, place a cigar on each plate and scatter berries over the top. Drizzle with a little pure cream and maple syrup.

Note   Use defrosted frozen berries if fresh are unavailable. Light cream and cottage cheese blend is a lower-fat alternative to mascarpone.

HAZELNUT CRISPBREADS

prep time: 5 minutes

cook time: 10 minutes

1 **tablespoon hazelnut paste (no added sugar)**
1 **tablespoon light cream and cottage cheese blend**
2 **teaspoons blackberry jam (no added sugar) or any sugar-free berry jam**
1 **piece soft flat bread**
1 **tablespoon chopped hazelnuts**
   macadamia nut oil/spray

Preheat oven to 350°F. Combine hazelnut paste, cream cheese and jam to form a smooth paste. Cut bread into triangles. Spread paste evenly over pieces and sprinkle with hazelnuts. Spray or drizzle with oil. Bake for 7–10 minutes until golden. Serve with tea or coffee.

WALNUT, CASTELLO AND DATE

prep time: 2 minutes

2   **tablespoons Blue Castello cheese (a soft, blue-veined Danish cheese)**
16   **walnut halves**
2   **dried dates, finely chopped**

Spread a fine layer of cheese over each walnut half and sprinkle with a little chopped date.

Note   For a low-carb lifestyle, dried fruit is usually forbidden but in such minute quantities for the occasional treat or impressive coffee companion, you can bend the rules a little. This combination was created with my Irish friend Ciara.

INDEX